Society of Illustrators, Inc.
128 East 63rd Street, New York, NY 10021

ISBN 0-942604-09-1

Library of Congress
Catalog Card Number 59-10849

Distributors to the trade in the United States:
Robert Silver Associates
307 East 37th Street, New York, NY 10016

Distributors to the trade in Canada:
General Publishing Co. Ltd., 30 Lesmill Road
Don Mills, Ontario, Canada M3B 2T6

Distributed outside U.S.A. and Canada by:
Hearst Publications International
1790 Broadway, New York, NY 10019

Publisher:
Madison Square Press, Inc.
10 East 23rd Street, New York, NY 10010

Editor: Arpi Ermoyan

Designer: Robert Anthony

Printed in Japan

PHOTO CREDITS: **Award Winners**/Brad Holland by Harold Sinclair
©1982; Teresa Fasolino by Vernon L. Smith, courtesy of Playboy. **Jurors**/
John Berg by David Kennedy, Nigel Holmes courtesy of Time Inc.; Brad
Thompson by Landshoff; Arthur Lidov by Alexandra Wool. **Hall of
Fame**/Robert Weaver by Todd Gangel.

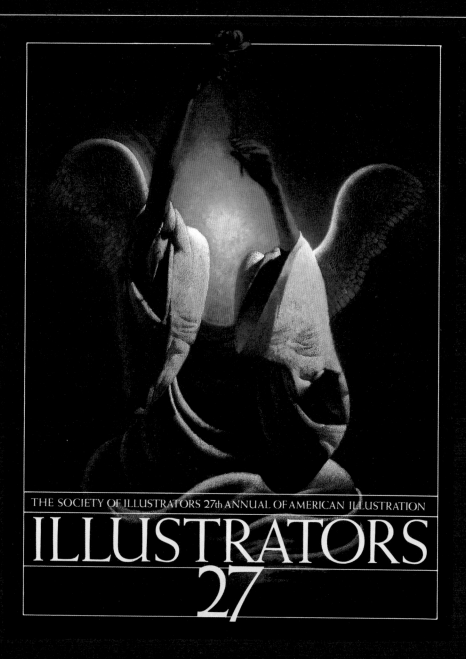

THE SOCIETY OF ILLUSTRATORS 27th ANNUAL OF AMERICAN ILLUSTRATION

ILLUSTRATORS
27

1/27

PUBLISHED FOR THE SOCIETY OF ILLUSTRATORS BY MADISON SQUARE PRESS, INC., NEW YORK
DISTRIBUTED BY ROBERT SILVER ASSOCIATES, NEW YORK

TABLE OF CONTENTS

PRESIDENT'S MESSAGE

Portrait by Robert Heindel

The Society of Illustrators is in its 27th year of publication of this book based on our annual show. Each year for the past 27 years we have contributed our bit to the history of illustration by recording it in our Annual. Now that we have been able to publish the whole book in full color, we can more closely approximate the impact of the show itself.

Each year the mix of paintings, drawings and sculpture has been more stunning, and the individual pieces more outstanding than the year before. This year is no exception. The level of excellence exhibited by the artists is extraordinary, and each year seems to be the apex, the absolute peak beyond which human capabilities cannot pass. Until, of course, we see what comes the following year, which, if this year's work is any standard to predict by, will be astounding.

An enormous amount of labor goes on behind the scenes to produce the show and the books. Our staff is kept busy for a good part of each year working on show-related tasks. The juries agonize for hours over thousands of high-quality entries in order to narrow down the list to a manageable size. Our Gallery Chairman and his committee of volunteers work diligently to hang the two halves of this large show. And finally, our Publications Chairman, designer and our publisher and his crew struggle to get the book together and out on time.

To all these people and to the artists whose works appear in this book, I can only offer my sincerest admiration and my heartfelt thanks.

D.L. Cramer
President, Society of Illustrators 1983-1985

i

CHAIRMAN'S MESSAGE

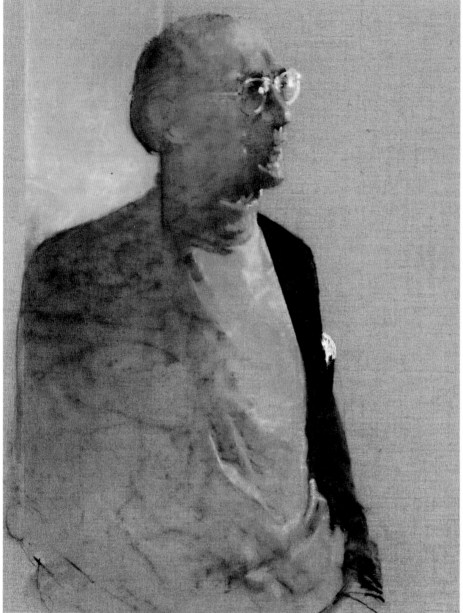

Arpi Ermoyan

Robert Anthony

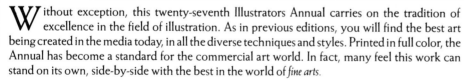

Without exception, this twenty-seventh Illustrators Annual carries on the tradition of excellence in the field of illustration. As in previous editions, you will find the best art being created in the media today, in all the diverse techniques and styles. Printed in full color, the Annual has become a standard for the commercial art world. In fact, many feel this work can stand on its own, side-by-side with the best in the world of *fine arts*.

The challenges are many for the men and women who contribute their talents in the quest for excellence, but the biggest challenge is for the creative "heads of state" who buy art and concern themselves with ideas. Today, as never before, the artist can make the difference between a million pages that are turned without a blink of the eye and one that makes the eye blink at its individuality.

I hope *you* will take into consideration the unlimited possibilities that exist today in the graphic arts field and stretch your own creativity in order to bring its uniqueness to the fore. As you thumb through the following pages, bear in mind how a single artist with a special talent can make a person stop and ponder. This volume, then, is an open door to art buyers around the world, to pursue that special talent and to bring inspiration to all artists.

Thanks to all who made this book possible — from those who created and submitted the entries, to the juries, to the publisher. Theirs is the real accomplishment.

Barnett Plotkin

Barnett Plotkin
Chairman, Illustrators 27

ILLUSTRATORS 27 ANNUAL EXHIBITION

Chairman / Barnett Plotkin
Associate Chairman / John Witt
Poster Artist / Barron Storey
Poster Designer/ Jerry McDaniel
Hanging Chairman / Wendell Minor
SI Staff / Terrence Brown, Executive Director,
Anna Lee Fuchs, Phyllis Harvey, Jennifer Paul,
Norma Pimsler, Fred Taraba

ILLUSTRATORS 27 ANNUAL BOOK

Editor / Arpi Ermoyan
Designer / Robert Anthony
Production Manager / Janet Weithas
Production Assistant / Jill Bossert
Advertising / Janet Weithas

Portraits by Robert Heindel

HALL OF FAME

As a dutiful Honorary President I am obeying a command to write a few words about the Hall of Fame awards. There are now many Hall of Fame awards in many disciplines including the performing arts. One of the first was the Baseball Hall of Fame in Cooperstown, New York, an annual event which began in 1938. It was natural that Babe Ruth was the first honoree, closely followed by Ty Cobb, Walter Johnson, Christy Mathewson and Honus Wagner.

In 1958 the Society of Illustrators similarly began selecting outstanding performers in the field of illustration. It is natural that Norman Rockwell heads the list, followed by Dean Cornwell and Harold Von Schmidt. In 1974 the Hall of Fame Committee deemed it important to include two posthumous awards annually in addition to a living contemporary illustrator. Leading this list is Charles Dana Gibson, N.C. Wyeth, Maxfield Parish and Howard Pyle. The latter is no relation to our Committee Chairman Willis Pyle who has steered the selections so long and so well.

I placed a call to the Director of the Baseball Hall of Fame and for the record, three of our awardees are represented in their permanent art collection with *Saturday Evening Post* cover originals: Norman Rockwell, John Falter and Stevan Dohanos.

Warmest congratulations to all honorees — past, present and future.

Stevan Dohanos
Stevan Dohanos
Honorary President

PREVIOUS HALL OF FAME WINNERS

Norman Rockwell 1958
Dean Cornwell 1959
Harold Von Schmidt 1959
Fred Cooper 1960
Floyd Davis 1961
Edward Wilson 1962
Walter Biggs 1963
Arthur William Brown 1964
Al Parker 1965
Al Dorne 1966
Robert Fawcett 1967
Peter Helck 1968
Austin Briggs 1969
Rube Goldberg 1970
Stevan Dohanos 1971
Ray Prohaska 1972
Jon Whitcomb 1973
Tom Lovell 1974
Charles Dana Gibson* 1974
N.C. Wyeth* 1974
Bernie Fuchs 1975
Maxfield Parrish* 1975
Howard Pyle* 1975
John Falter 1976
Winslow Homer* 1976
Harvey Dunn* 1976
Robert Peak 1977
Wallace Morgan* 1977
J.C. Leyendecker* 1977
Coby Whitmore 1978
Norman Price* 1978
Frederic Remington* 1978
Ben Stahl 1979
Edwin Austin Abbey* 1979
Lorraine Fox* 1979
Saul Tepper 1980
Howard Chandler Christy* 1980
James Montgomery Flagg* 1980
Stan Galli 1981
Frederic R. Gruger* 1981
John Gannam* 1981
John Clymer 1982
Henry P. Raleigh* 1982
Eric (Carl Erickson)* 1982
Mark English 1983
Noel Sickles* 1983
Franklin Booth* 1983
Neysa Moran McMein* 1984
John LaGatta* 1984
James Williamson* 1984

presented posthumously

HALL OF FAME 1985

Charles Marion Russell*
Arthur Burdett Frost*
Robert Weaver

HALL OF FAME COMMITTEE

Chairman / Willis Pyle
Past Presidents of the Society:
Walter Brooks, Harry Carter
Stevan Dohanos, Tran Mawicke
Charles McVicker, John A. Moodie
Howard Munce, Alvin J. Pimsler
Warren Rogers, William Schneider
Shannon Stirnweis, David K. Stone
John Witt

Charles Marion Russell was born in Oak Hill near St. Louis, Missouri, on March 19, 1864. The Russells were an affluent industrial family with ancestral ties to the early West. Charlie's great uncles had been fur traders in a vast area bordering the upper Missouri River. Perhaps the most famous was William Bent, who with Jim Bridger and Kit Carson explored the Rockies and became the first permanent settler in what is today the state of Colorado. Family talk of Bent's adventures stimulated the imagination of young Russell. The lure of the Old West took hold of him at an early age.

Since the days of Lewis and Clark, St. Louis had been the gateway to the West. It was headquarters for the fur trade and jumping-off point for pioneers seeking a new life, fame and fortune. The riverfront traffic was a beehive of activity, and its sights and sounds were a magnetic attraction to Russell. Hooky from school was the result. A rebellious lad, he had a marked aversion to formal education. Instead of arithmetic and English, his school notebooks were crammed with sketches of cowboys and Indians, replete with chaps, war bonnets, Colts and Winchesters, painted ponies and the like. In early March of 1880, a few days before his 16th birthday, Charlie left school for good and — with tacit permission and help from his parents — headed for Montana Territory. From that time on, the West was to be his heart and home; it remained so until his death in Great Falls on October 24, 1926.

In the wilderness of Montana, Russell became companion to trapper and hunter, friend of Indian and cowboy. He lived much of the life he depicted on canvas and modeled in clay and wax. The "cowboy artist," as he was to become known, had little art instruction. As with a great many artists, he was entirely self-taught. His student years were the summer cowcamps, night wrangling, riding herd or telling tall tales around the night fires. The long winters were spent in trappers' cabins and cowtown saloons, where he sketched and painted.

After a brief sojourn sheepherding in the Judith Basin country, a friendship with a hunter and trapper named Jake Hoover brought Charlie into close contact with big-game animals. For two years he accompanied Hoover on hunting expeditions in the high country, furnishing meat for the tables of scattered settlers in the region.

CHARLES M. RUSSELL
(1864 - 1926)

Big game was plentiful in the 1880s. Gaining invaluable knowledge by observing the various species in their natural environments, he made hundreds of sketches that served him well in future works. He became an expert in animal anatomy, due chiefly to the experience gained when skinning out Hoover's kills. To this day Charles Russell is acknowledged as the finest sculptor of wildlife in western Northern America.

Montana was also Indian country, and Russell's contact with the Blackfoot, Piegan, Crow, Sioux, Cree and Flathead tribes was frequent. He learned to speak a bit of Piegan and could "talk sign" well enough to get along with any of the Plains Indians. In 1888 he stayed six months with the Blood Indians of Canada, a primitive branch of the Blackfoot tribe. He learned their customs, habits and ways of life, and developed a deep understanding and heart-felt appreciation of the Indian philosophy.

After his stay with Hoover, Charlie got his first job night wrangling. Wherever he went, he sketched and modeled the daily events of ranch life: roping, branding, bronc breaking, fun and frolic. For ten years, from 1882 to 1892, he led the revelous life of a cowboy, drifting up and down Montana with the cattle herds. During these years, Charlie was typically generous with his work — as all cowboys were wont to be — and placed little monetary value

on it. A goodly number of early Russells were bartered to feed a friend or buy a round of drinks. He would, on occasion, make a gift of a painting to an acquaintance who showed a particular liking for it.

Friends continually urged him to devote all of his energies to painting, but he couldn't resist being the carefree cowboy, however tough and rigorous such an existence might be. But the barbed-wire fence was closing the open range, and free grass was disappearing. The time had finally come to take up the paintbrush permanently.

In 1895, Russell met Nancy Cooper and married her the following year. Due primarily to her influence, Charlie was better able to schedule his creative time. Nancy handled the sales, business contacts and commissions, and there is little doubt that she was responsible for his ultimate financial success.

His pictures soon started to appear on the pages of the popular sporting periodicals of the day. Such magazines as *Recreation, Western Field and Stream, Field and Stream, Outing* and *Sports Afield* were his early showcases. By the turn of the century, Russell's reputation as a Western artist and illustrator was well-established. In time, his paintings would illustrate articles in *Scribner's, McClures, The Saturday Evening Post* and *Leslie's Weekly.* The opportunity for book illustration also attracted Russell's talents. Notable among a long list of titles were *Chip of the Flying U, The Virginian* and *Indian Why Stories.* Charlie Russell was also an extremely colorful writer, and his series of *Rawhide Rawlins Stories* are today classics of Western literature.

However lucrative the field of publishing might have been, Russell's main objective was painting for his own personal satisfaction. His paintings found enthusiastic response from leading galleries and collectors throughout the United States. Exhibitions in Canada and England made his name well known in art circles on two continents.

During his lifetime, this gifted artist produced a considerable catalog of work: some 2500 paintings and drawings plus several hundred individual bronze statues and wax models. No other American artist has portrayed the old West so vigorously or has known it so intimately.

Douglas Allen, *Artist-Consultant,*
Sports Afield magazine

"In the Wake of the Buffalo Runners"

A. B. Frost's parents, John Frost and Sarah Ann Burdett, were married in 1830 in a ceremony conducted by Ralph Waldo Emerson. Of the ten children born of this union, only three survived beyond the late 1860s. John Frost was a Harvard graduate and served as headmaster and professor at various schools in Boston and Philadelphia. He eventually devoted his time exclusively to writing histories and biographies of which over 300 were published. A.B. Frost's brother became the owner of *Godey's Ladies Book*, his sister was a successful author and most famous of all the relatives was a distant cousin, the renowned poet, Robert Frost. A distinguished and talented family, indeed!

As a struggling young lithographer, A.B. Frost was suddenly catapulted into fame at the age of 23 when he illustrated a book, *Out of the Hurly Burly*, with nearly 400 drawings. They were done in pen-and-ink on wood, one of the few methods which could be reproduced in those days, and were of necessity drawn in simple line. The book sold over a million copies, including translations into foreign languages, and was an instant sensation. Two years later he started working with watercolors and gouache, showing great skill in this medium as well as in pen-and-ink.

In 1877 he went to London for a year of study and work, then returned to study portraiture with Thomas Eakins at the Pennsylvania Academy of Fine Arts. There he met and fell in love with Emily Phillips, the daughter of a wealthy industrialist. Emily was an accomplished artist and published illustrator in her own right. They were married on October 19, 1883, and moved to Huntington, Long Island. Four years later, anticipating their first child, the Frosts moved to larger quarters in Pennsylvania and spent a good portion of their summers at the New Jersey shore. Frost did many watercolors and oils of the local beaches, dunes and duck marshes which he enjoyed so much. His ability to depict the mood, detail and authenticity of sporting scenes eventually

ARTHUR BURDETT FROST
(1851 - 1928)

earned him the reputation of the "Sportsman's Artist."

In 1890, expecting another addition to the family, the Frosts bought a large country estate, appropriately named "Moneysunk," in Convent Station, New Jersey. The sixteen years they lived in that house were the happiest of their lives — years during which he did his most important and memorable work. The house, built late in the 18th century on a campsite of the Continental Army and used as a station on the "underground railroad," still stands and is a historical point of interest.

In 1906 Frost moved his family to Paris where he entered both sons in the Academie Julian. Soon after settling in, young Arthur met Matisse, Picasso and others of the modern school and dropped out of the Academie to join Matisse's newly formed art class. A.B. Frost, bitterly disappointed that his son was not

following the traditional school, was dealt a final blow when Arthur Frost, Jr., died suddenly in 1917 of a tubercular hemorrhage just four days before his thirtieth birthday. Frost never completely recovered from the shock and grief of his son's death. Because the other son, John, had also contracted tuberculosis while in Europe, the Frosts moved to the warm, dry climate of California in 1919 to help him recover. They settled in Pasadena, where John became a successful painter during the 1920s.

A.B. Frost's career spanned nearly 50 years of continuous work during which he turned out a steady stream of drawings, paintings, sketches and illustrations for the leading magazines of the day. Because he was colorblind it was necessary for his wife or one of his sons to label the colors of his palette. Despite this impaired vision (or possibly because of it) he had a remarkable sense of color values.

For almost ten years he worked side-by-side at *Harper's* with Edwin Austin Abbey, Frederic Remington, Howard Pyle (at whose wedding he was best man) and numerous other well-known artists. While Remington and Charles Russell depicted the American West, Frost was pictorially recording the Eastern scene: farmers, barnyards, plantation life, creatures and birds of the marshes and the men who hunted them.

He illustrated the works of Mark Twain and Joel Chandler Harris. He created the images of Tom Sawyer, Huck Finn, Uncle Remus and all their friends as we see them today in our mind's eye. His drawings for Harris's immortal "Uncle Remus" series truly earned his reputation as a master draftsman and helped establish B'rer Rabbit as one of the classic characters in American literature.

A.B. Frost died in his sleep on June 22, 1928, at the age of 77 and is buried in Laurel Hill Cemetery, Philadelphia.

Arpi Ermoyan

"The Four Seasons," one of a series, 1906

In a time of unbridled self-interest and slick professionalism, Robert Weaver stands apart. For his whole career as an illustrator he has stood firmly planted in the truth. In reaction to illustration that caters to a desire to see ourselves in a good light — as represented by artists like Norman Rockwell — or that creates a mythology born of Hollywood, he feels the need "for a more accurate way of seeing life." He says, "You don't need to deplore it, or expose it ... just document it," and quotes Flannery O'Connor: "to portray poverty is to condemn it."

Conversation with Weaver — an imposing, rangy and highly articulate man — is scattered with quotations and sly humor. But one is struck most by the element of caring within him. He cares about the inequities in our society and the dangers to the environment. He cares deeply about good drawing and about drawing the right things. He also cares about preserving illustration: "It's not that I think these things are great masterpieces. I think anything that gets into print in a national magazine is of historical interest." More so, he says, than gallery art — in which he, as an artist, has had no interest — a forum where critics dictate the marketplace. Illustration is not subject to the whim of critics, but is a living representation of the culture. It was not illustrators, however, who influenced Weaver. In fact, he came to the profession by chance.

Born in Pittsburgh in 1924, he experienced the Annual Carnegie International and, like millions, devoured *The Saturday Evening Post.* The excellent drawings of Hal Foster's *Prince Valiant* and Burne Hogarth's *Tarzan* also impressed the young Weaver. He studied at the Carnegie Institute, then in New York at the Art Students League and at the Metropolitan Museum of Art, "the best art school with the best faculty." Later, when he fell in love with the heavenly light of Venice, he continued his studies at the Accademia Delle Belle Arti.

He arrived in New York with a portfolio of mural sketches which he took to *Town & Country.* He had the very charming idea that he would like a job as a color expert advising art directors. Instead, Tony Mazzola offered him several manuscripts to illustrate. Weaver's

ROBERT WEAVER
(b. 1924)

knowledge of the business was so scant that when Tony spoke of "not bleeding," the artist thought he mustn't depict violence, and "avoiding the gutter" indicated he shouldn't show the seamier side of life. His work was accepted and Weaver became an illustrator, in spite of himself.

"It's this thing of seeing your work in a magazine. My God, I was down at five o'clock in the morning to see the first copies of *Town & Country* being unbaled. It's addictive ... you see your work in a big stack of magazines and you want to see it again. I like the idea of the printed page — the accessibility, the availability, the two-sidedness of a page."

His greatest activity was from the late '50s through the '70s when he worked for people like Henry Wolf at *Esquire,* Leo Lionni at *Fortune,* and Cipe Pineles at *Charm* and *Seventeen* — art directors he admires greatly for the freedom they allowed. The art directors at *Sports Illustrated, Playboy, Life, Look,* and *Columbia Records,* among others, saw the wisdom of giving Weaver full reign. The result was acclaim and awards, including a Gold Medal from the Society in 1964.

A source of inspiration for Weaver was the cinema: early Orson Welles and the post-war Italians — Rossellini and DeSica — who "knocked [him] out of [his] aisle seat onto the floor." They showed him "you could look at real things ... an old negro lady sitting on a bench on the Williamsburg Bridge, or the ordinary people of Rome, and you can make art out of it. There is drama in the most ordinary things if you just pay close attention." Ben Shahn was an artist in whose work Weaver saw the truthful representation of life.

It is this sense of obligation to see clearly and record faithfully that Robert Weaver has been trying to instill in his students. He has taught as a visiting faculty member at Syracuse University and for over fifteen years at the School of Visual Arts, which hosted a Retrospective of his work in 1977. In a field he feels is too glamourized and "like TV commercials," he is trying to reassert the journalistic aspect of illustration. "I tell my students to stop being conceptual and get back to looking at things, at the details ... to observe light and color and pattern. I tell them to take risks, to get their feet into the water. They've got to overcome fear." He sends them out to record the life on 42nd Street, the homeless in Grand Central Station, and the action in the St. Marks baths. He is rewarded with real art drawn from real life.

Because he believes the day of the magazine as an outlet for the illustrator is gone, for him, it is the book which offers a much broader surface on which to work. A work-in-progress is a large-format book about New York City. His love of the turnable page and the juxtaposition of various images and ideas is dramatically wedded here. On one page the subway meets the swaying trees of the Bronx, on another Jason Robards rehearses under Times Square neon to show the city where contrasts occur at breakneck speed.

Robert Weaver is the artist as socially aware being. He is an artist who takes the responsibility of using line, color, and form as tools to tell us, with intelligence — not cleverness — what goes on in the world around us.

Jill Bossert

"Roach Powder in the Maple Walnut"

HAMILTON KING AWARD 1985

The Hamilton King Award is presented annually for the finest illustration in the Annual Exhibition done by a member of the Society of Illustrators. The selection is made by former recipients of this award. The 1985 winner is Attila Hejja for his painting, *Lightship*, done for the National Aeronautics and Space Administration.

HAMILTON KING AWARD WINNERS

ATTILA HEJJA
(b. 1955)
Interviewed by Terry Brown

TERRY BROWN: Attila, congratulations on winning both a Gold Medal and the Hamilton King Award for your painting, *Lightship*.

ATTILA HEJJA: Thank you. Honestly, both awards were a pleasant surprise.

TB: That night launch of the Shuttle must have been dramatic.

AH: Very much so. I was with the press in a site over 3 miles away. At about midnight, a fierce thunderstorm with violent lightning passed over the launch site. Suddenly it ended and a quiet calm settled in. It turned into a heavy, hazy night. When the Shuttle lifted off at 2 a.m., it lit up the sky most dramatically.

TB: We're all curious as to how you developed the vantage point for this piece.

AH: Actually, it was constructed from a few elements. The perspective is from 1500 feet aloft and half a mile away from the Shuttle. I had flown an OV10 on an Air Force assignment the prior year. We flew over what was to be the launch site where I took reference photos. That was all I needed to create the landscape.

TB: Were you able to take effective photographs during the launch?

AH: Yes, but it was a stroke of chance. The press photographers and I were all guessing on exposure. I also did some quick sketches. Together they were the final pieces of the image.

TB: Compared to many of your other NASA paintings, this work stresses less of the hardware.

AH: That's true. It is more of a landscape, an interpretation of lighting and cloud structure. It was fun to get involved in the physics of the image.

TB: What was your art training that led you to these achievements?

AH: I was fortunate to have had a superior teacher in Harold Stevenson. I apprenticed with him for four years on a daily basis. He had been one of the few students of Norman Rockwell, and an illustrator before taking up teaching.

TB: What were the methods he stressed?

AH: Harold taught the classic academic approach, heavy into anatomy and figure drawing. It has given me a strong background in the basics which I've been able to build on.

TB: And your family background?

AH: My family moved from Budapest, where I was born, and settled on Long Island. We spoke Hungarian at home so I had trouble with English. I think in the long run it made me more visually oriented. I began at a young age to draw and to create images of futuristic landscapes and flying machines.

TB: How did you end up in the illustration market?

AH: It was through another illustrator, Harry Schaare. I had tried my hand at portraits and gallery work for awhile. And then I met Harry. I was about 20. He told me what to expect in this field and convinced me that I could do it.

TB: Were your early works in the aerospace field?

AH: Yes, my timing was good. This was just after the movie "Star Wars" and my style and subject matter were perfect. I was doing paperback science fiction almost exclusively.

TB: Til, let's talk about the NASA program. How does one participate?

AH: The artists are invited by NASA. Robert Schulman, who directs the program, deserves a great deal of credit for maintaining the quality of the art. I was invited to view the night Shuttle launch as my sixth launch. The first Shuttle assignment in 1981 was by invitation of the U.S. Air Force.

TB: Do you feel the NASA Art Program serves a valid purpose?

AH: Yes, definitely. The NASA charter calls for it "to disseminate information on space." Through the body of work created by the artists a lot of the untold story, missing on photographs, is documented. As an artist, I see this documentary style as being in the same tradition as Homer's work during the Civil War and Remington's paintings of the West.

TB: You must also feel rewarded to be a part of history.

AH: Rewarded, yes, but also inspired. I feel that I have to do something extraordinary, to really excel.

"Lightship." Collection of National Aeronautics and Space Administration

TB: Have you ever been involved in flight yourself?

AH: I did learn to fly at age fifteen and have been in F16's and F106's for the USAF Art Program. I even flew F5F's for the Royal Saudi Air Force.

TB: That must have been an unusual trip.

AH: It certainly was. The Saudis were overwhelmed and most grateful. I was part of a group of artists commissioned by Northrop Corporation to document the activities of the Saudi Air Force.

TB: Have you ever been in a spacecraft?

AH: Only at the Johnson Space Center in Houston. That was the flight simulator.

TB: Would you want to fly in the Shuttle?

AH: Who wouldn't? I remember an observation by Eugene Cernan after an early space flight. He said he was able to see in one view where all of history had taken place and it made him feel small. That really affected me.

TB: And what do you think the future holds for you?

AH: For now I'm very happy illustrating. It has a certain vitality that I enjoy. Eventually, though, I would like to explore serious science fiction. By that I mean what hasn't yet been done. I have some ideas about the road to civilization and what the right path is to take us where we should be.

TB: Are you optimistic that we will follow the right path?

AH: Yes, we all want to live. If we begin to think more as a species and not as individual segments, it will change our outlook.

TB: The Hamilton King Award is an important honor. Again, my congratulations.

AH: Thanks. I was quite pleased, both for myself and for NASA. These awards elevate the stature of NASA art and further the idea of documentary art as being important. In a true sense it is the most valid rendering of history that exists.

SOCIETY OF ILLUSTRATORS MUSEUM OF AMERICAN ILLUSTRATION

The Society of Illustrators Museum of American Illustration continues to be a great visual forum for illustrators past and present.

Some of the outstanding group exhibits in the 1984-85 season were:

America's Great Women Illustrators 1850-1950, which represented 40 artists with a total of 90 pieces. The hundred year span included artists from the Golden Age, such as Jessie Wilcox Smith and Violet Oakley, to post-World War II illustrators Dorothy Hood and Lorraine Fox.

The Charles E. Cooper Studio, now considered famous for the many talented artists it represented in years past, provided a fascinating exhibition with a look at the early works of Jon Whitcomb, Herb Tauss, Joe Bowler, Coby Whitmore and Bernard D'Andrea, to name but a few.

The Annual Air Force Art Show once again demonstrated the very high caliber of work done by Society members for the permanent collection of the United States Air Force. Our thanks to Keith Ferris for doing a superb job as chairman of this important project!

Individual artists presented a wide spectrum of personal views in their respective one-man shows. From Alvin Pimsler's mastery of portraiture to Lou Myers' perpetually witty pen, one could gather much insight into the artist's development of style and character.

Other shows that created a constant flow of traffic through the Museum's galleries were those of Daniel Schwartz, portraits of Arthur William Brown (1881-1966) by Society members, Lou Glanzman, Joe Mendola's artists, Constantin Alajalov, Hotel Barmen's Association Calendar, Al Parker Memorial Exhibition, Paul Davis, Westport Artists, Stevan Dohanos and the Gilbert Stone Memorial (1940-1984).

The Museum strives to provide a diverse overview of the American illustrator. The exhibitions of the past year have been excellent examples in making that view a clearer one!

Wendell Minor
Chairman, Exhibition Committee

AMERICA'S GREAT WOMEN ILLUSTRATORS 1850-1950

Jessie Willcox Smith, "Mother and Child," cover illustration for *Dream Blocks* by Aileen Cleveland, 1908. Courtesy of Mr. & Mrs. Benjamin Eisenstat

Violet Oakley, "Portrait of Jessie Willcox Smith." Courtesy of Mr. & Mrs. Benjamin Eisenstat

SOCIETY OF ILLUSTRATORS MUSEUM OF AMERICAN ILLUSTRATION

Ellen Bernhard Thompson Pyle, "The Immigrants," illustration for *Story of the Revolution* by Paul Leicester, 1899. Courtesy of Brandywine River Museum.

U.S. AIR FORCE ART

Jim Sharpe, "Mission Accomplished." Courtesy, U.S. Air Force Art Collection

CHARLES E. COOPER STUDIO

Joe Bowler, "First Love, the Second Time." Collection of Society of Illustrators Museum of American Illustration

Coby Whitmore, "Love is a Bargain," illustration for *Ladies' Home Journal,* 1947. Collection of Society of Illustrators Museum of American Illustration

Bernie D'Andrea, "The Widow," illustration for *Good Housekeeping* magazine, 1962. Collection of Society of Illustrators Museum of American Illustration

THE ILLUSTRATOR IN AMERICA 1880-1980

Planning an exhibition of the magnitude of a hundred years of American Illustration was a daunting task, particularly the scheduling of its opening with the publication date of *The Illustrator in America 1880-1980* on November 7, 1984. Both projects were being pursued simultaneously, which had some advantages, but also created a lot of time pressure.

Fortunately, it all was accomplished and all else was forgotten in the pleasure of seeing together so many of the great classic works of art by Howard Pyle, N.C. Wyeth and Edwin Austin Abbey, as well as many previously unseen, but also great, works by artists such as Rose O'Neill, Samuel Nelson Abbott, Walter H. Everett, Guy Hoff, Edmund F. Ward, Frank Walter Taylor and Anna Whelan Betts.

The original works exhibited were — wherever possible — those reproduced in the book.

Otherwise, the examples chosen were the finest available. For these, we had many generous lenders, both individuals and institutions, to thank. Among them were the Brandywine River Museum, the Delaware Art Museum, The New Britain Museum of American Art, the Society of Illustrators Museum of American Illustration, Illustration House, Nabisco Brands, American Cyanamid Corporation, Mr. and Mrs. Benjamin Eisenstat, Mr. and Mrs. Ray Sacks of Sacks Fine Arts, Elizabeth Athern and June Tabor, Mr. and Mrs. Charles Matz, Morris Weiss, Richard Kravitz, Andrew Sordoni III, Bob and Joan Wale, Willis Pyle, Mort Künstler, the Lockwood Family Collection, Janet and Arthur Weithas, Andra Kustin, Mrs. Paul Rabut, Mr. and Mrs. Davies, Bevi Bullwinkel and Walter Granville-Smith III, Mrs. John Held, Jr., Mac Fisher, Frederic R. Gruger, Jr., Judy and Alan Goffman, Mrs.

Henry Pitz, J. B. Rund, Les Mansfield, Mrs. Amos Sewell, Mrs. Haddon Sundblom, Mrs. Earl Oliver Hurst, Murray and Carol Tinkelman, Mrs. Jacqueline Fowler, the exhibiting artists and many others.

The pictures were expertly hung by Wendell Minor and his crew and arranged by visual affinity rather than the usual historical progression. This allowed for many interesting juxtapositions and provided a fresh look at the works. Excellent publicity was created by Janet and Arthur Weithas and Madison Square Press. All of the logistics were expertly coordinated through the good offices of Terry Brown and Fred Taraba. It was a pleasure and a privilege to have worked with all of the above.

Walt and Roger Reed
Illustration House

Walter H. Everett, illustration for *Ladies' Home Journal*, 1909. Collection of Illustration House

Guy Hoff, cover illustration for *The Saturday Evening Post.* Collection of Illustration House

Leo and Diane Dillon, cover illustration for *Ashanti to Zulu - African Traditions* by Margaret Musgrove, 1976

Dana Taylor, Paier College of Art

T he Society of Illustrators Annual Student Competition is undoubtedly one of the most rewarding areas in which we can dedicate valuable time. There's an inspiring spirit coming not only from the students but from the teachers, the jurors, and the committee members as well.

We all well remember our days of struggle, and to see such a testimony to talent and effort be so richly rewarded is thanks enough for any time and effort spent on this annual competition.

Over 120 college-level institutions were represented by 4,800 entries and the selection of 161 works was exhibited in the Society's Museum of American Illustration April 29 through May 17, 1985.

This year, forty thousand dollars in grants were presented through the support of the Lila Acheson Wallace Fund, The Starr Foundation, The Book-of-the Month Club, Hearst Magazines, Jellybean Photographics and many private donors. The schools of the students who have been selected for these awards will receive matching grants from Hallmark Cards, Inc.

Our commendation, also, to the illustration departments throughout the country for providing the forum for instruction. And finally, our support and heartiest commendation to *all* students for their perseverance in light of stiff competition not only in this competition but also awaiting them in the marketplace.

We wish you all *great* success!

Eileen Hedy Schultz
Chairperson, Scholarship Committee

Quang Ho, Colorado Institute of Art

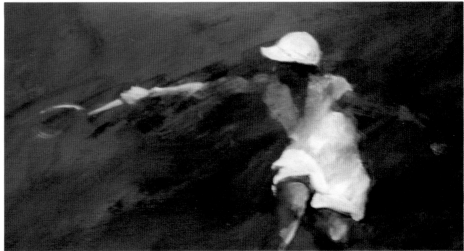

Robert Wisnewski, Rhode Island School of Design

JURY

DOUG JOHNSON
Chairman
Illustrator

VIVIENNE FLESHER
Illustrator

BERNIE FUCHS
Illustrator

HOWARD KOSLOW
Illustrator

ANITA KUNZ
Illustrator

LEN LEONE
Formerly Art Director,
V.P., Bantam Books

KEN PETRETTI
Art Director,
ABC Television

IRENE RAMP
Art Director,
Time magazine

NEIL STUART
Art Director,
Viking/Penguin
Adult Books

AWARD WINNERS

BRAD HOLLAND
Gold Medal

MATT MAHURIN
Gold Medal/Silver Medal

MALCOLM T. LIEPKE
Gold Medal

GUY BILLOUT
Silver Medal

ROBERT M. CUNNINGHAM   **JAMES E. TENNISON**

EDITORIAL

Artist: MATT MAHURIN

4

Artist: BRAD HOLLAND
Art Director: Tom Staebler / Kerig Pope
Magazine: Playboy

GOLD MEDAL

5

Artist: MATT MAHURIN
Art Director: Louise Kollenbaum
Magazine: Mother Jones

8

Artist: GUY BILLOUT
Art Director: Judy Garlan / Terry Brown
Magazine: The Atlantic Monthly

SILVER MEDAL

Artist: MARK CHICKINELLI   Art Director: Greg Paul   Magazine: Sunshine

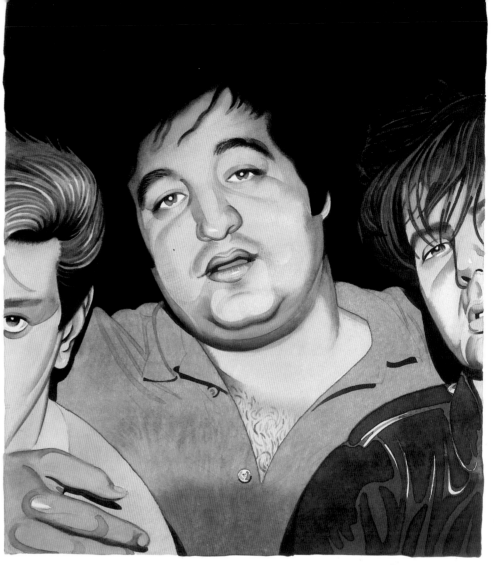

10
Artist: JEFFREY SMITH
Art Director: Thomas Ruis
Magazine: New York Daily News

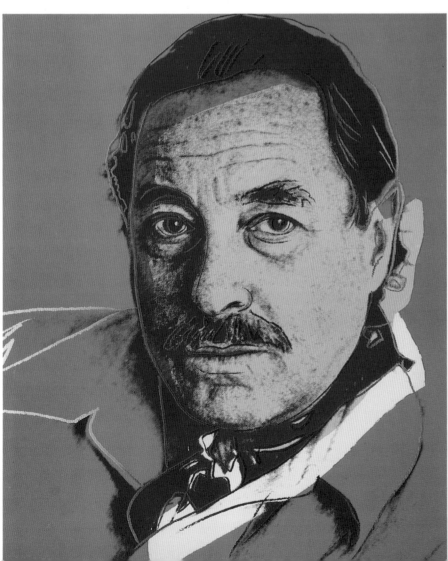

11
Artist: ANDY WARHOL
Art Director: Tom Staebler / Kerig Pope
Magazine: Playboy

12
Artist: KEN JOUDREY
Art Director: Mare Earley
Magazine: H.F.D., The Weekly Home Furnishings Newspaper

13
Artist: JULIAN ALLEN
Art Director: Ruth Ansel
Magazine: ᵔ .nity Fair

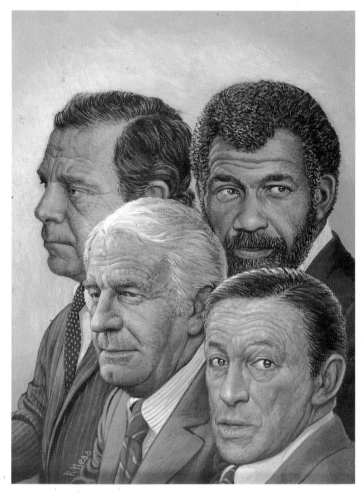

14
Artist: RICHARD HESS
Art Director: Jerry Alten
Magazine: TV Guide

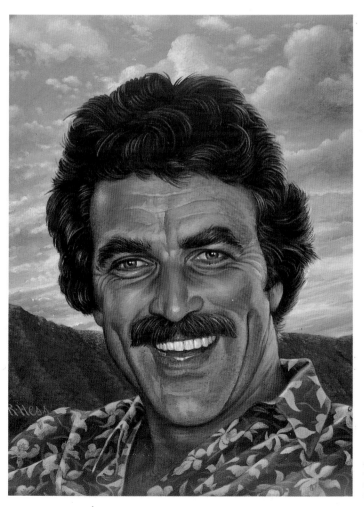

15
Artist: RICHARD HESS
Art Director: Jerry Alten
Magazine: TV Guide

18
Artist: R.B. KITAJ
Art Director: Rudy Hoglund
Magazine: Time

16
Artist: ALAN E. COBER
Art Director: Fred Woodward
Magazine: Texas Monthly

17
Artist: VIVIENNE FLESHER
Art Director: Bett McLean
Magazine: The Best of Business

19
Artist: MEL ODOM
Art Director: Tom Staebler / Kerig Pope
Magazine: Playboy

20
Artist: CRISTINE MORTENSEN
Art Director: Eleanor O. Leishman
Magazine: Women's Sports

21
Artist: MARK PENBERTHY
Art Director: Fo Wilson / Marlowe Goodson
Magazine: Essence

22
Artist: EVERETT DAVIDSON

23
Artist: CAMILLE PRZEWODEK

24
Artist: BARBARA NESSIM
Art Director: Barbara Nessim
Magazine: Communication World

25
Artist: LESLIE CABARGA
Art Director: Margery Peters
Magazine: Fortune

26
Artist: CATHY HULL
Art Director: Joe McNeill / John Arocho
Magazine: Forum

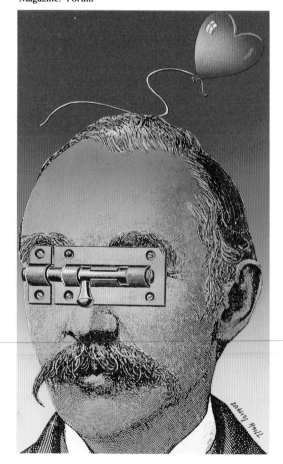

Artist: KUNIYA   Art Director: Derek Ungless   Magazine: Rolling Stone

28
Artist: ROBERT RISKO
Art Director: Tom Staebler / Theo Kouvatsos
Magazine: Playboy

29
Artist: EDWARD SOREL
Art Director: Rudy Hoglund
Magazine: Time

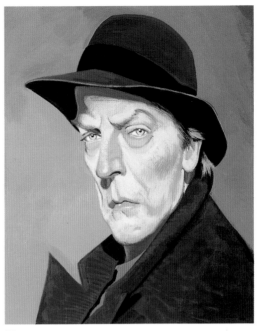

30
Artist: ROBERT RISKO
Art Director: Marc Balet
Magazine: Interview

31
Artist: WILLIAM CONE

32
Artist: KENT BARTON   Art Director: Kent Barton   Magazine: Miami Herald

DONT LET THE STARS GET IN YOUR EYES!!!

THEY'LL BURN YOUR HEAD RIGHT OFF.

33
Artist: GARY PANTER
Art Director: Louise Kollenbaum
Magazine: Mother Jones

34
Artist: JULIAN ALLEN   Art Director: Ruth Ansel   Magazine: Vanity Fair

35
Artist: ALAN E. COBER
Art Director: Robert Best
Magazine: New York

36
Artist: BUDDY HICKERSON
Art Director: James Noel Smith
Magazine: Westward

37
Artist: STEVE BRODNER
Art Director: Tom Staebler/Theo Kouvatsos
Magazine: Playboy

38
Artist: IAN POLLACK
Art Director: Derek Ungless
Magazine: Rolling Stone

39
Artist: WILLIAM BASSO

40
Artist: MARSHALL ARISMAN
Art Director: Louise Kollenbaum
Magazine: Mother Jones

41
Artist: BILL NELSON
Art Director: Jann Alexander
Magazine: Washington Post

42
Artist: MARSHALL ARISMAN
Art Director: James Noel Smith
Magazine: Westward

43

Artist: ANITA KUNZ
Art Director: Blair Caplinger
Magazine: Tables

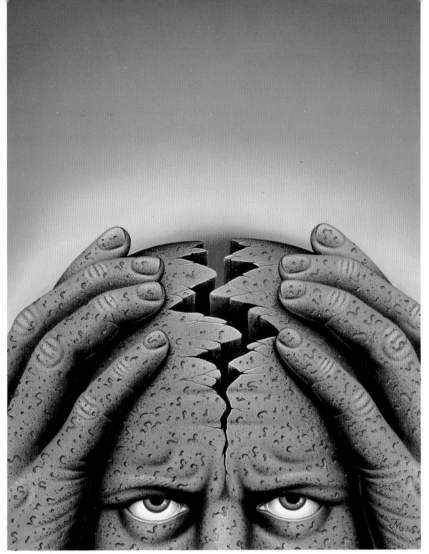

44
Artist: JAMES MARSH
Art Director: Rudy Hoglund
Magazine: Time

45
Artist: JEFF LARAMORE
Art Director: Jeff Laramore
Magazine: Indianapolis

46
Artist: GARY KELLEY
Art Director: Gary Bernloehr
Magazine: Florida Trend

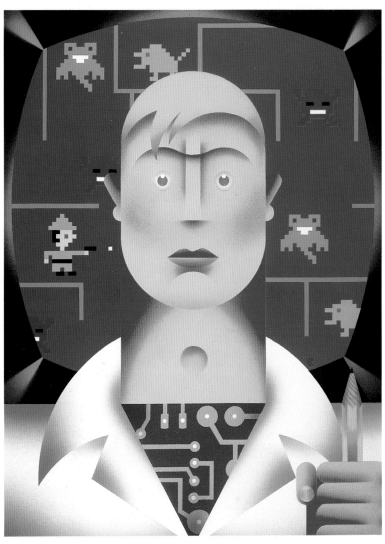

47
Artist: JOSÉ CRUZ
Art Director: Joe Connolly
Magazine: Boy's Life

48
Artist: DAVID COULSON
Art Director: Richard Altemus / Rick Stark
Magazine: Family Weekly

49
Artist: LOU BROOKS
Art Director: Derek Ungless
Magazine: Rolling Stone

50
Artist: LOU BROOKS
Art Director: C.J. Cacchione
Magazine: Audio

51
Artist: KENNETH KRAFCHEK   Art Director: Barbara Maiolatesi   Magazine:

52
Artist: ROBERT HUNT   Art Director: Ed Guthero   Magazine: Listen

53
Artist: ROBERT GANTT STEELE
Art Director: Alison Brown
Client: Pittman Learning, Inc.

54
Artist: MARK PENBERTHY
Art Director: Ralph Stello
Magazine: U.S. Pharmacist

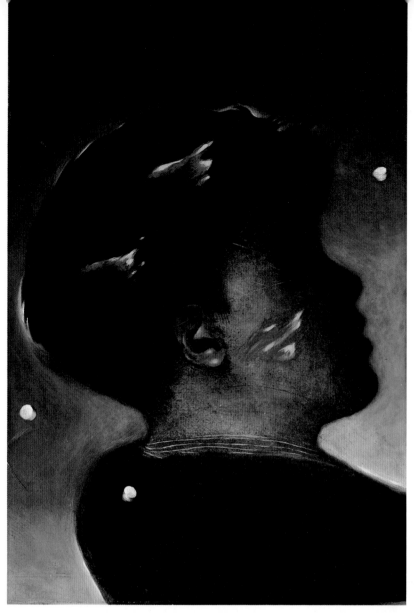

55
Artist: WILSON McLEAN
Art Director: Les Goodman
Magazine: Psychology Today

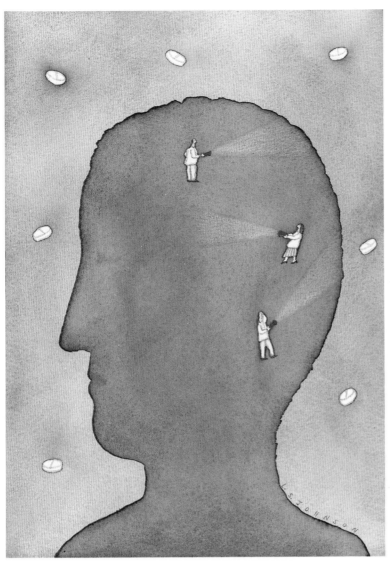

56

Artist: LONNI SUE JOHNSON
Art Director: Tina Adamek
Magazine: Postgraduate Medicine

57

Artist: DENNIS WHEELER
Art Director: Forbes Linkhorn
Magazine: American Journal Of Nursing

58
Artist: TOM CURRY   Art Director: Fred Woodward   Magazine: Texas Monthly

59
Artist: JUDY PEDERSEN
Art Director: Barbara Lish
Magazine: Avenue

60
Artist: LYNDA BARRY
Art Director: Sally Ham
Magazine: Campus Voice Biweekl

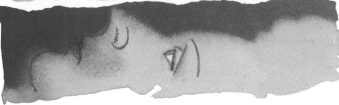

61
Artist: JEFFREY SMITH
Art Director: Fred Woodward
Magazine: Texas Monthly

62
Artist: FRANCES JETTER
Art Director: Ronn Campisi
Magazine: Boston Globe

63
Artist: GOTTFRIED HELNWEIN
Art Director: Derek Ungless
Magazine: Rolling Stone

64
Artist: TOM DOLPHENS
Art Director: Randy Wyrick
Magazine: Kansas City Star

65
Artist: LOU BROOKS
Art Director: Barbara Koster / Marcia Wright
Magazine: TWA Ambassador

66

Artist: JANET TURNER
Art Director: Donald H. Duffy
Magazine: Reader's Digest

67

Artist: NORMAN ADAMS   Art Director: Victor J. Closi   Magazine: Field & Stream

68
Artist: DOUGLAS SMITH
Art Director: Ronn Campisi
Magazine: Boston Globe

69
Artist: TOM DOLPHENS
Art Director: Bill Sikes
Magazine: Kansas City Star

Artist: BUDDY HICKERSON   Art Director: James Noel Smith   Magazine: Westward

71
Artist: NOVLE ROGERS
Art Director: James Noel Smith
Client: Dallas Times Herald

72
Artist: STEVE PIETZSCH
Art Director: James Noel Smith
Magazine: Westward

73
Artist: ELWOOD H. SMITH
Art Director: Carol Carson
Magazine: Let's Find Out

74
Artist: DOUG JOHNSON
Art Director: Rudy Hoglund
Magazine: Time

75
Artist: WENDY BURDEN
Art Director: Steven Hoffman
Magazine: Vantage Point, Issues In American Arts

77
Artist: DENISE WATT
Art Director: Eduardo Boetsch
Magazine: Pennzoil's Perspectives

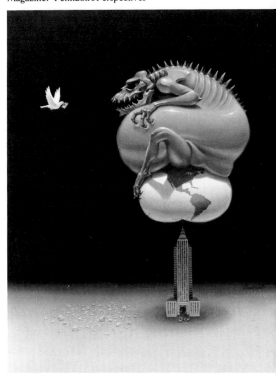

76
Artist: JÖZEF SUMICHRAST
Art Director: Jane Palecek
Magazine: International Wild Life

78

Artist: JOHN D. DAWSON   Art Director: Howard E. Paine   Magazine: National Geographic

79

Artist: JOHN D. DAWSON   Art Director: Howard E. Paine   Magazine: National Geographic

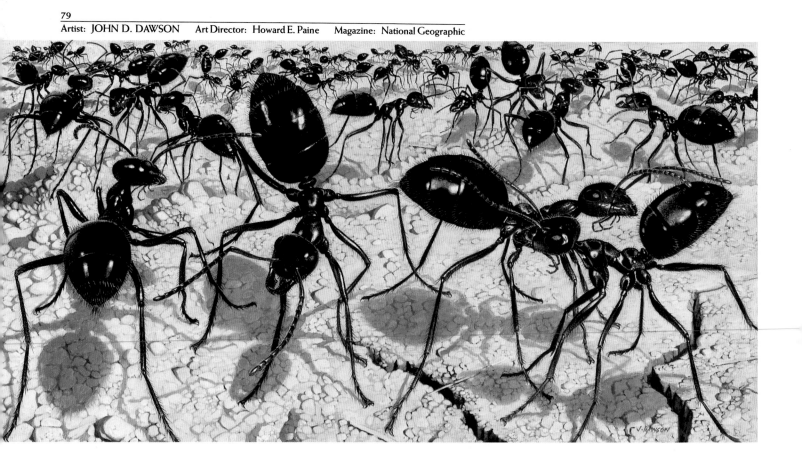

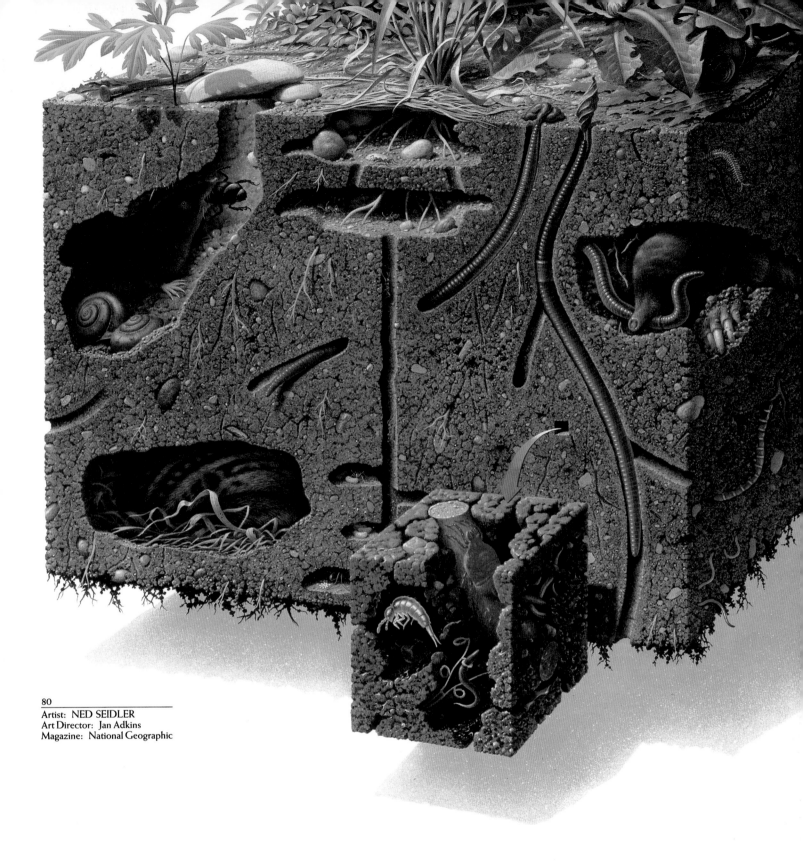

Artist: NED SEIDLER
Art Director: Jan Adkins
Magazine: National Geographic

81

Artist: BRAD HOLLAND   Art Director: Judy Garlan   Magazine: The Atlantic Monthly

82
Artist: TERRY ALLEN
Art Director: Margery Peters
Magazine: Fortune

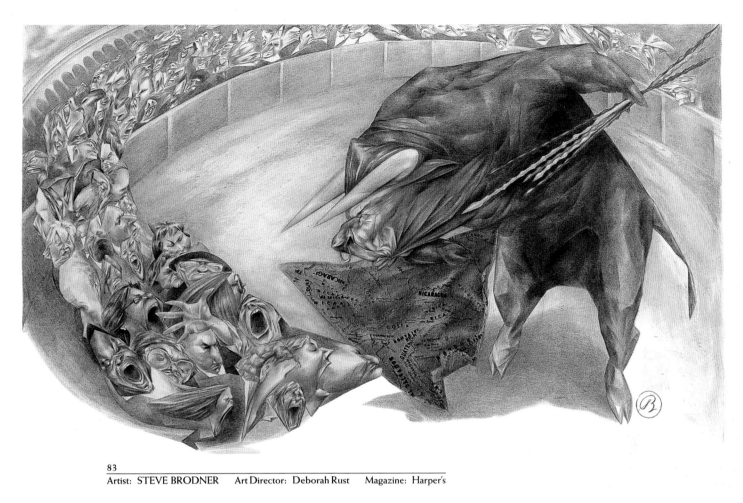

83

Artist: STEVE BRODNER   Art Director: Deborah Rust   Magazine: Harper's

84

Artist: JAMES ENDICOTT   Art Director: Judy Garlan   Magazine: The Atlantic Monthly

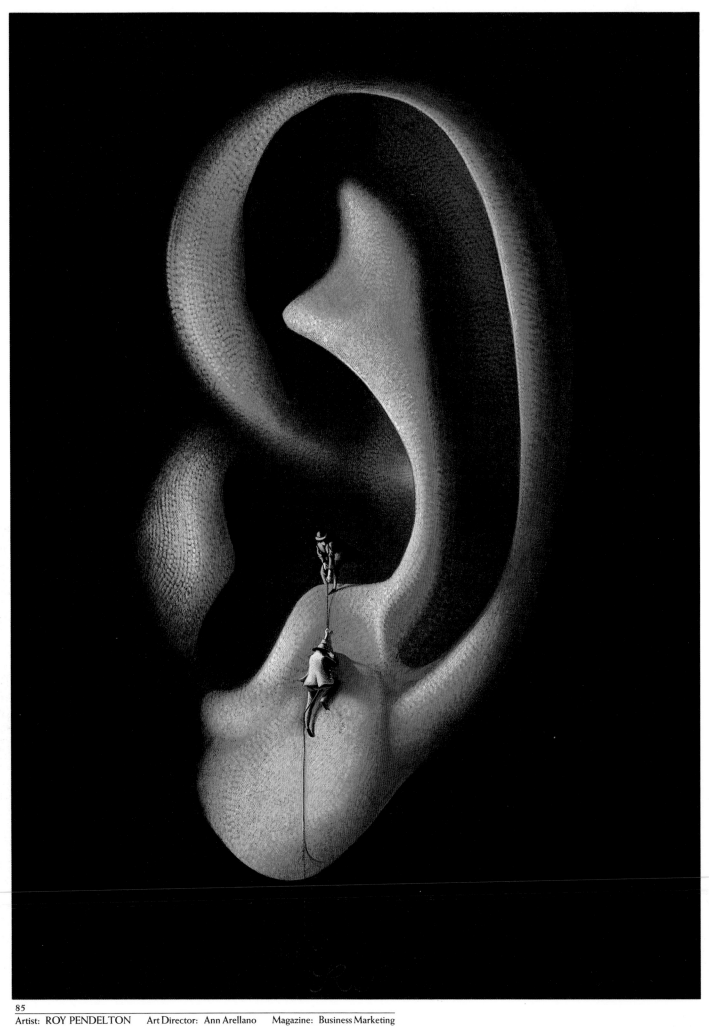

85
Artist: ROY PENDELTON   Art Director: Ann Arellano   Magazine: Business Marketing

86
Artist: BRALDT BRALDS
Art Director: Michael Valenti
Magazine: Science Digest

88
Artist: MARIAN C. ZACHAROW

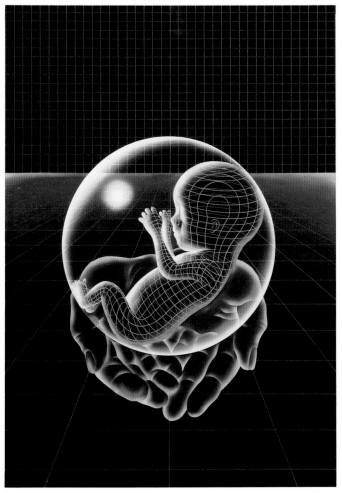

87
Artist: CAROL GILLOT
Art Director: Rudy Hoglund
Magazine: Time

89
Artist: CHRIS VAN ALLSBURG
Art Director: Judy Garlan
Magazine: The Atlantic Monthly

90
Artist: CHRIS VAN ALLSBURG
Art Director: Judy Garlan
Magazine: The Atlantic Monthly

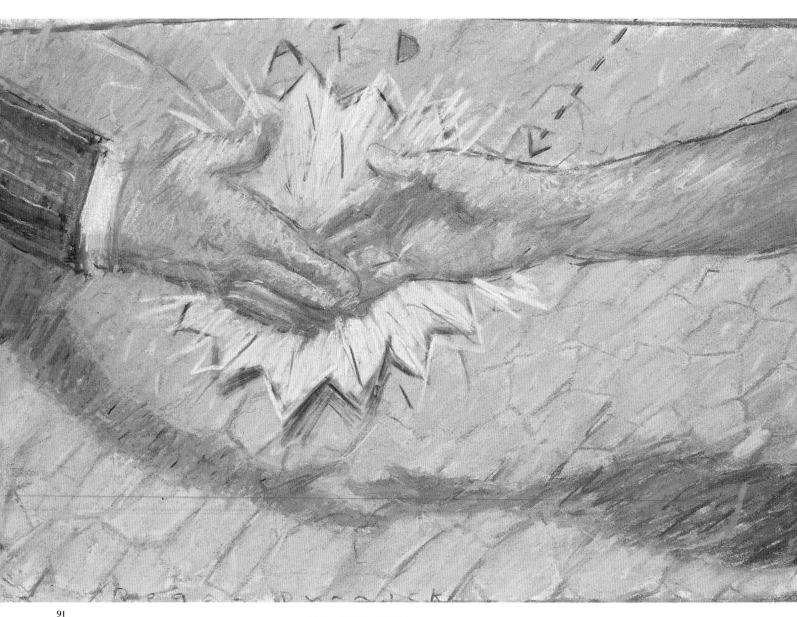

91
Artist: REGAN DUNNICK   Art Director: Fred Woodward   Magazine: Texas Monthly

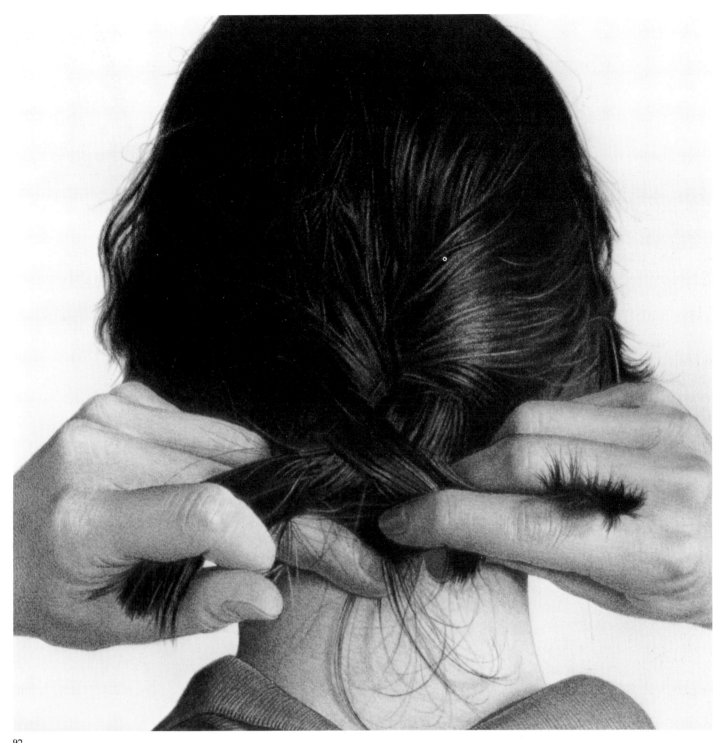

92
Artist: RALPH GIGUERE   Art Director: Judy Garlan   Magazine: The Atlantic Monthly

93
Artist: JUDY CLIFFORD
Art Director: Nina Ovryn
Magazine: Review

94
Artist: JUDY CLIFFORD
Art Director: Nina Ovryn
Magazine: Review

95
Artist: JUDY CLIFFORD
Art Director: Nina Ovryn
Magazine: Review

96
Artist: JUDY CLIFFORD
Art Director: Nina Ovryn
Magazine: Review

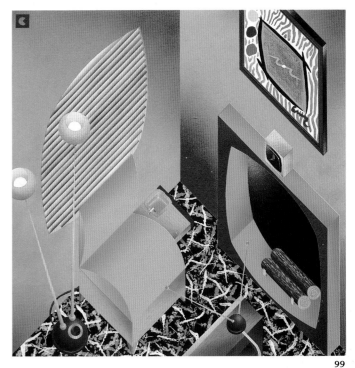

98

Artist: JOSÉ CRUZ
Art Director: Fred Woodward
Magazine: Texas Monthly

99

Artist: JOSÉ CRUZ
Art Director: Judy Garlan
Magazine: The Atlantic Monthly

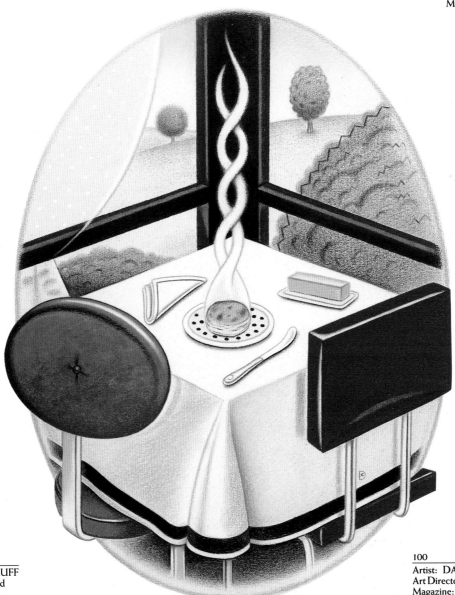

97

Artist: THOMAS WOODRUFF
Art Director: Fred Woodward
Magazine: Texas Monthly

100

Artist: DAVE CALVER
Art Director: Fred Woodward
Magazine: Texas Monthly

101
Artist: CATHY BARANCIK
Art Director: Patricia Von Brachel
Magazine: New York

102
Artist: CATHY BARANCIK
Art Director: Ronn Campisi
Magazine: Boston Globe

103
Artist: CATHY BARANCIK
Art Director: Ken Newbaker
Magazine: Philadelphia

Artist: WENDY BURDEN   Art Director: Kati Korpijaakko   Magazine: Mademoiselle

105
Artist: AJIN NODA
Art Director: Rudy Hoglund
Magazine: Time International

106
Artist: STEVEN GUARNACCIA
Art Director: Ronn Campisi
Magazine: Boston Globe

107
Artist: BARBARA NESSIM   Art Director: Rosslyn A. Frick   Magazine: Byte

Artist: THEO RUDNAK
Art Director: Greg Paul
Magazine: Sunshine

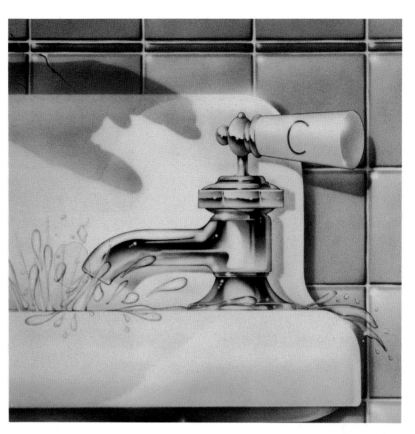

110
Artist: MERLE NACHT
Art Director: Barbara Koster
Magazine: TWA Ambassador

108
Artist: DEAN WILLIAMS
Art Director: Ed Guthero / Dean Williams
Magazine: Listen

111
Artist: JIM SPANFELLER
Art Director: Barry L.S. Mirenburg
Magazine: Croton Review

112
Artist: MAURICE LEWIS
Art Director: Eduardo Boetsch
Client: Pennzoil Company

113
Artist: G. ALLEN GARNS
Art Director: John Casado
Client: Volvo

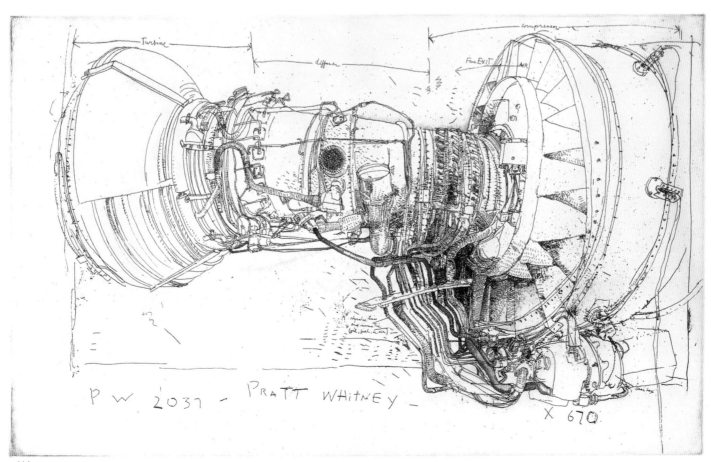

P W 2037 – PRATT WHITNEY –

X 670

114
Artist: ALAN E. COBER   Art Director: Elton Robinson   Magazine: The Lamp

115
Artist: GREG SPALENKA
Art Director: Laura Lamar / Deborah Stairs
Magazine: San Francisco Focus

116
Artist: KENT WILLIAMS

117
Artist: GREG SPALENKA
Art Director: Gary Mele
Magazine: MS.

118
Artist: EDITH VONNEGUT
Art Director: Tom Staebler / Kerig Pope
Magazine: Playboy

119
Artist: BRAD HOLLAND   Art Director: Derek Ungless   Magazine: Rolling Stone

120
Artist: BRAD HOLLAND
Art Director: Barbara Solowan / Bernadette Gilcen
Magazine: City Woman

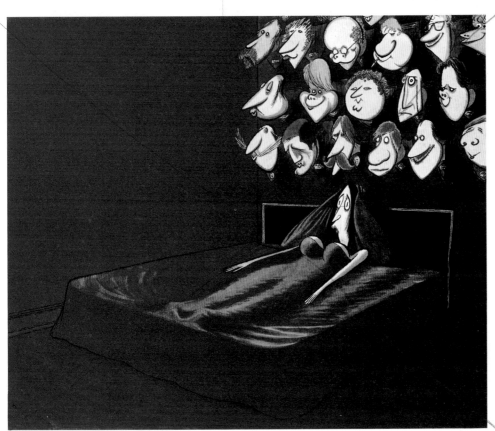

121
Artist: ARNOLD ROTH
Art Director: Rudy Hoglund
Magazine: Time

122
Artist: ANITA KUNZ
Art Director: Tom Staebler / Kerig Pope
Magazine: Playboy

123
Artist: GARY KELLEY
Art Director: Fred Woodward
Magazine: Texas Monthly

Artist: MATT MAHURIN   Art Director: Wayne Fitzpatrick / Joyce Black   Magazine: Science 84

125
Artist: RUSSELL D. JONES
Art Director: Alfred Zelcer
Magazine: Philadelphia

126
Artist: MATT MAHURIN
Art Director: Louise Kollenbaum
Magazine: Mother Jones

127
Artist: MATT MAHURIN
Art Director: Fred Woodward
Magazine: Texas Monthly

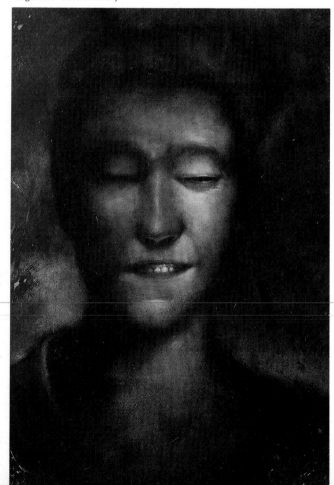

128
Artist: DAGMAR FRINTA
Art Director: Mary Challinor / Joyce Black
Magazine: Science 84

129
Artist: ED SOYKA
Art Director: Richard Altemus / Rick Stark
Magazine: Family Weekly

130

Artist: RANDALL ENOS   Art Director: Ronn Campisi   Magazine: Boston Globe

131
Artist: PATTY DRYDEN
Art Director: Greg Paul
Magazine: Sunshine

132
Artist: BOYD HANNA
Art Director: Carol Buchanan
Magazine: The Artist's Magazine

Pierre was new in town and had never really caught anything before

133
Artist: ALEXA GRACE
Art Director: Fred Woodward
Magazine: Texas Monthly

134
Artist: STEVE SHOCK   Art Director: Ken Ovryn   Magazine: Outside

135
Artist: GREG SPALENKA

136
Artist: CATY BARTHOLOMEW

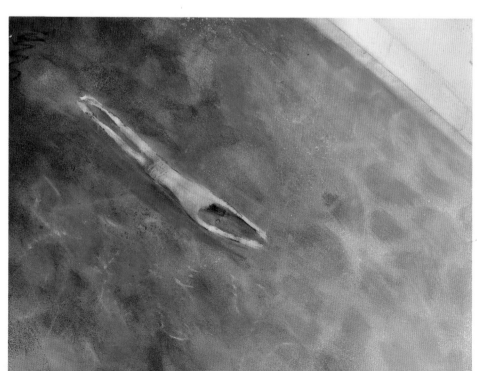

137
Artist: MICHELLE BARNES

138
Artist: TERRY WIDENER
Art Director: Diane Marince / Mike Fuld
Magazine: American Way

139
Artist: FRED OTNES
Art Director: Joe Connolly
Magazine: Boy's Life

140

Artist: ROBERT M. CUNNINGHAM   Art Director: Harvey Grut   Magazine: Sports Illustrated

141

Artist: ROBERT M. CUNNINGHAM   Art Director: Harvey Grut   Magazine: Sports Illustrated

142
Artist: ROBERT ANDREW PARKER   Art Director: Robert Best   Magazine: New York

143
Artist: BRAD HOLLAND
Art Director: Louise Kollenbaum
Magazine: Mother Jones

144
Artist: DANIEL MAFFIA
Art Director: Veronique Vienne
Magazine: West

145
Artist: PAUL MELIA

146
Artist: EDWARD SOREL   Art Director: Jay Purvis   Magazine: Gentleman's Quarterly

147
Artist: ROBERT RISKO
Art Director: Barbara Koster
Magazine: TWA Ambassador

148
Artist: MARC ROSENTHAL
Art Director: Margery Peters
Magazine: Fortune

149
Artist: BERNIE FUCHS
Art Director: Norman S. Hotz
Magazine: Reader's Digest

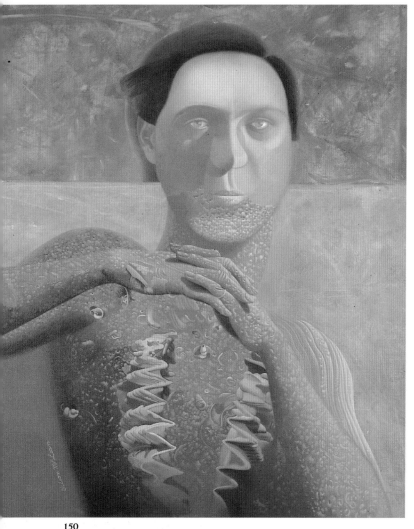

150
Artist: WILSON McLEAN
Art Director: Tina Adamek
Magazine: Postgraduate Medicine

151
Artist: DAVE CALVER
Art Director: Barbara Koster
Magazine: TWA Ambassador

152
Artist: DICK KREPEL
Art Director: Jerry Demony
Client: Mobil Oil Corporation

Artist: MARK PENBERTHY   Art Director: Mary Zisk / Mitch Shostak   Magazine: PC

Artist: HENRIK DRESCHER   **Art Director:** John Cohoe   **Magazine:** Geo

155
Artist: VIVIENNE FLESHER
Art Director: James Noel Smith
Magazine: Westward

156
Artist: NOVLE ROGERS
Art Director: Broc Sears
Client: Dallas Times Herald

157
Artist: SARA SCHWARTZ
Art Director: Amy Sussmanheit
Magazine: Art Direction

158
Artist: MICHAEL GARLAND
Art Director: Kenneth Surabian
Magazine: Datamation

159
Artist: FRANCES JETTER
Art Director: Thomas Ruis / Janet Froelich
Magazine: New York Daily News

Artist: ANTHONY RUSSO   Art Director: Donna Albano   Magazine: The Baltimore Sun

Artist: ANDRZEJ DUDZINSKI   Art Director: Wayne Fitzpatrick / Joyce Black   Magazine: Science 84

162
Artist: MARK MAREK
Art Director: Derek Ungless
Magazine: Rolling Stone

163
Artist: STAN McCRAY
Art Director: James Noel Smith
Magazine: Westward

165
Artist: DAVID LEE CSICSKO
Art Director: Bob Post
Magazine: Chicago

166
Artist: SUSAN J. CURTIS
Art Director: Kati Korpijaakko
Magazine: Mademoiselle

164
Artist: SUSAN J. CURTIS
Art Director: Frank Tagariello
Magazine: Geo

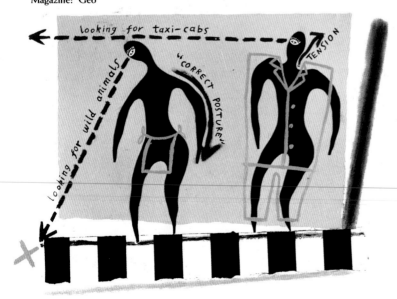

Artist: BARBARA NESSIM   Art Director: Melissa Tardiff   Magazine: Town & Country

168
Artist: CAROL WALD
Art Director: Theo Kouvatsos
Magazine: Playboy

169
Artist: JOHN RUSH
Art Director: Virginia Murphy-Hamill
Magazine: Today's Office

Artist: SANDRA FILIPUCCI   Art Director: Tina Adamek   Magazine: Postgraduate Medicine

171
Artist: DAGMAR FRINTA
Art Director: Marcia Wright
Magazine: TWA Ambassador

173
Artist: THOMAS WOODRUFF
Art Director: Louise Kollenbaum
Magazine: Mother Jones

172
Artist: PAUL YALOWITZ

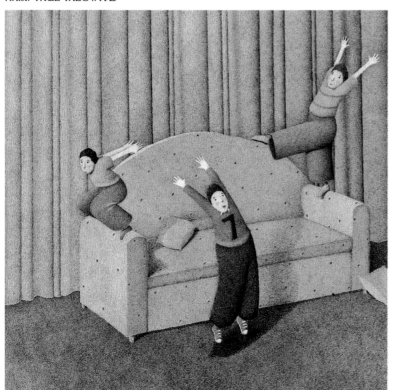

174
Artist: ED KOSLOW
Art Director: Skip Williamson
Magazine: Playboy

175
Artist: J.P. SCHMELZER
Art Director: J.P. Schmelzer / Jack Slotag
Magazine: Chicago Tribune
Weekend Tempo

Artist: TERRY ALLEN
Art Director: Ronn Campisi / Marty Braun
Magazine: Boston Globe Sunday

Artist: NOVLE ROGERS   Art Director: Broc Sears   Client: Dallas Times Herald

Artist: GUY BILLOUT   Art Director: Judy Garlan   Magazine: The Atlantic Monthly

179
Artist: GUY BILLOUT
Art Director: Marcia Wright
Magazine: TWA Ambassador

180
Artist: GUY BILLOUT
Art Director: Judy Garlan
Magazine: The Atlantic Monthly

181
Artist: ELWOOD H. SMITH
Art Director: Andrew Epstein
Magazine: The Best Of Business

182
Artist: ELWOOD H. SMITH
Art Director: Fred Woodward
Magazine: Texas Monthly

183
Artist: SEYMOUR CHWAST
Art Director: Hans-Georg Pospischil
Magazine: Frankfurt Allgemeine

184
Artist: EDWARD GOREY
Art Director: Jerry Alten
Magazine: TV Guide

185
Artist: EDWARD GOREY   Art Director: Lloyd Ziff   Magazine: House & Garden

186
Artist: RALPH GIGUERE
Art Director: Judy Garlan
Magazine: The Atlantic Monthly

187
Artist: ANITA KUNZ
Art Director: Judy Garlan
Magazine: The Atlantic Monthly

188
Artist: LONNI SUE JOHNSON
Art Director: Amy Bogert
Magazine: American Bookseller

189
Artist: LONNI SUE JOHNSON
Art Director: Linda Evans
Client: 13-30 Corporation

190

Artist: MICHEL GUIRE VAKA   Art Director: Blair Caplinger   Magazine: Tables

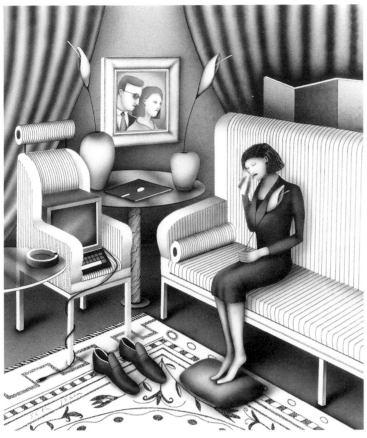

191
Artist: SETH JABEN
Art Director: Thomas Ruis
Magazine: New York Daily News

192
Artist: GARY ZAMCHICK
Art Director: Sally Ham
Magazine: The Wallpaper Journal

193
Artist: STEVE JOHNSON
Art Director: David Hadley
Client: Minneapolis Star & Tribune

194

Artist: TERESA FASOLINO   Art Director: Tom Staebler / Bruce Hansen   Magazine: Playboy

195
Artist: NICHOLAS GAETANO
Art Director: Lee Ann Jaffee
Magazine: Meetings & Conventions

196

Artist: ROBERT M. CUNNINGHAM   Art Director: Harvey Grut   Magazine: Sports Illustrated

MATTELSON

198
Artist: THOMAS AQUINAS DALY
Art Director: Gary Gretter
Magazine: Sports Afield

199
Artist: CHARLES REID
Art Director: Gary Gretter
Magazine: Sports Afield

197
Artist: MARVIN MATTELSON
Art Director: Bob Eichinger
Client: St. Regis Paper

200

Artist: ARTHUR SHILSTONE   Art Director: De Courcy Taylor   Magazine: Gray's Sporting Journal

201

Artist: FRANKLIN JONES   Art Director: De Courcy Taylor   Magazine: Gray's Sporting Journal

202
Artist: RICK McCOLLUM
Art Director: Alice Borenstein
Magazine: Amtrak Express

203
Artist: JEAN LEON HUENS
Art Director: J. Robert Teringo
Magazine: National Geographic

204
Artist: LINDA GIST   Art Director: Modesto Torre   Magazine: McCall's

Artist: WILLIAM LOW
Art Director: Richard Altemus / Rick Stark
Magazine: Family Weekly

Artist: JOHN BERKEY   Art Director: Wm. A. Motta   Magazine: Road & Track

208
Artist: FRANCES JETTER
Art Director: Richard Altemus / Rick Stark
Magazine: Family Weekly

209
Artist: WILLIAM LOW
Art Director: Thomas Ruis
Magazine: New York Daily News

207
Artist: JEFFREY SMITH
Art Director: Ken Smith
Magazine: Campus Voice Biweekly

210
Artist: ROBERT HEINDEL
Art Director: Harvey Grut
Magazine: Sports Illustrated

211
Artist: DENNIS ZIEMIENSKI
Art Director: Harvey Grut
Magazine: Sports Illustrated

212
Artist: BOB DORSEY   Art Director: Greg Paul   Magazine: Cleveland Plain Dealer

213
Artist: DENNIS ZIEMIENSKI
Art Director: Harvey Grut
Magazine: Sports Illustrated

214
Artist: JUDY CLIFFORD
Art Director: Nina Ovryn
Magazine: Review

Artist: MICHAEL McGAR
Art Director: Fred Woodward
Magazine: Texas Monthly

215
Artist: DENNIS ZIEMIENSKI
Art Director: Harvey Grut
Magazine: Sports Illustrated

216
Artist: SCOTT REYNOLDS
Art Director: Riki Allred
Magazine: Northeast

217
Artist: SCOTT REYNOLDS
Art Director: Riki Allred
Magazine: Northeast

Michael McGar © 84

219
Artist: KIM DREW
Art Director: Dan Junsa / John Twohey
Magazine: Chicago Tribune

220
Artist: RAFAL OLBINSKI
Art Director: Lee Ann Jaffee
Magazine: Meetings & Conventions

221
Artist: ALEX GNIDZIEJKO
Art Director: Modesto Torre
Magazine: McCall's

222
Artist: SCOTT GORDLEY
Art Director: Scott Gordley
Magazine: American Artist

Artist: LANE SMITH
Art Director: Ellen Blissman
Magazine: Money

223
Artist: KENT BARTON
Art Director: Kent Barton
Magazine: Miami Herald

225
Artist: ANTHONY RUSSO
Art Director: Donna Albano
Client: The Baltimore Sun

226
Artist: SUE COE
Art Director: Louise Kollenbaum
Magazine: Mother Jones

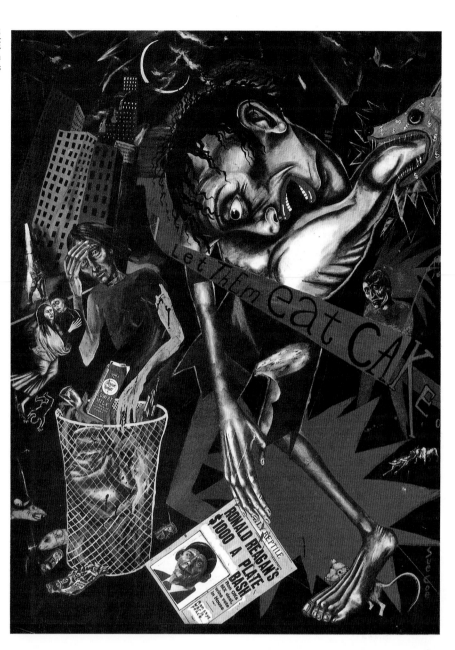

227
Artist: TOM LULEVITCH
Art Director: Judy Garlan
Magazine: The Atlantic Monthly

229
Artist: K. MERCEDES McDONALD
Art Director: Barbara Koster
Magazine: TWA Ambassador

230
Artist: SETH JABEN
Art Director: Tina Adamek
Magazine: Postgraduate Medicine

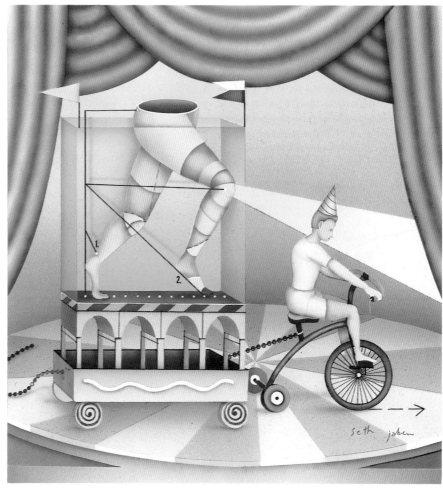

228
Artist: TOM SCIACCA

GERARD HUERTA
Chairman
Graphic Designer

CATHY BARANCIK
Illustrator

REGAN DUNNICK
Illustrator

NIGEL HOLMES
Executive Art Director,
Time magazine

ARTHUR LIDOV
Illustrator

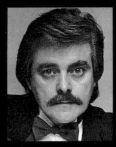

WILSON McLEAN
Illustrator

WOODY PIRTLE
Graphic Designer

BRADBURY THOMPSON
Graphic Designer

ROBERT WEBSTER
Graphic Designer

AWARD WINNERS

JOHN COLLIER
Gold Medal / Silver Medal

MICKEY PARASKEVAS
Silver Medal

BOOK

Artist: JOHN COLLIER
Art Director: Dale Pollekoff

232
Artist: JOHN COLLIER
Art Director: Dale Pollekoff
Publisher: Time-Life Books

SILVER MEDAL

233
Artist: MICKEY PARASKEVAS
Art Director: Marshall Arisman

SILVER MEDAL

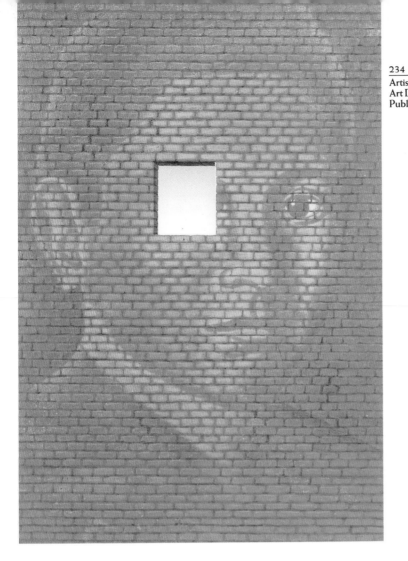

234
Artist: FRED MARCELLINO
Art Director: Louise Fili
Publisher: Pantheon Books

235
Artist: KATHERINE MAHONEY
Art Director: Char Lappan
Publisher: Little, Brown & Company

Artist: RICK McCOLLUM   Art Director: William Gregory   Publisher: Reader's Digest

Artist: LOUIS S. GLANZMAN   Art Director: Len Leone   Publisher: Bantam Books

238
Artist: WENDELL MINOR
Art Director: Robert D. Reed
Publisher: Holt, Rinehart & Winston

239
Artist: MARK LANGENECKERT   Art Director: Dale Pollekoff / Louis Klein   Publisher: Time-Life Books

241
Artist: DICK LUBEY
Art Director: Carl Zollo
Client: Rochester Sesquicentennial Committee

242
Artist: NEIL WALDMAN
Art Director: Connie Ftera
Publisher: Prentice-Hall Company

240
Artist: HERBERT TAUSS
Art Director: Michael Mendelsohn
Publisher: The Franklin Library

243
Artist: PETER FIORE
Art Director: Michael Mendelsohn
Publisher: The Franklin Library

244
Artist: WENDY K. POPP
Art Director: Robert Mitchell
Publisher: McGraw Hill

245
Artist: FLOYD COOPER
Art Director: William Mathison
Publisher: The Economy Company

246
Artist: LEONARD BASKIN
Art Director: Denise Cronin
Publisher: Knopf / Pantheon Books for Young Readers

247
Artist: LEONARD BASKIN
Art Director: Denise Cronin
Publisher: Knopf / Pantheon Books for Young Readers

248
Artist: LEONARD BASKIN
Art Director: Denise Cronin
Publisher: Knopf / Pantheon Books for Young Readers

249
Artist: VIVIENNE FLESHER   Art Director: Michael Mendelsohn   Publisher: The Franklin Library

250
Artist: ANITA KUNZ
Art Director: Judith Loeser
Publisher: Vintage Books

251
Artist: MARSHALL ARISMAN
Art Director: Dale Pollekoff / Louis Klein
Publisher: Time-Life Books

252
Artist: JOHN MARTINEZ
Art Director: Louise Fili
Publisher: Pantheon Books

253
Artist: BASCOVE
Art Director: Louise Fili
Publisher: Pantheon Books

254
Artist: JIM CHAMBERLAIN

255
Artist: KAREN KATZ   Art Director: Sara Eisenman   Publisher: Alfred A. Knopf, Inc.

256
Artist: RICHARD ROSS   Art Director: Neil Stuart   Publisher: Viking Press

257
Artist: MELANIE MARDER PARKS
Art Director: Keith Sheridan
Publisher: Random House

258
Artist: KEVIN KING
Art Director: Michael Mendelsohn
Publisher: The Franklin Library

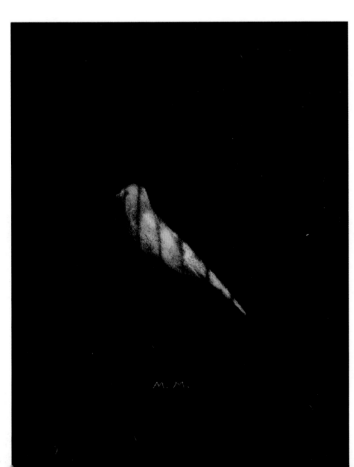

259
Artist: MATT MAHURIN
Art Director: Diana Klemins
Publisher: Dell Publishing

260
Artist: JOHN JUDE PALENCAR
Art Director: Dale Pollekoff / Louis Klein
Publisher: Time-Life Books

261
Artist: BRALDT BRALDS   Art Director: Diana Klemins   Publisher: Doubleday & Company, Inc.

262
Artist: WAYNE ANDERSON
Art Director: Dale Pollekoff / Louis Klein
Publisher: Time-Life Books

263
Artist: MARTIN PATE

264
Artist: FRANK K. MORRIS
Art Director: Frank K. Morris
Publisher: Freundlich Books

265
Artist: MICHAEL HAGUE
Art Director: David Tommasino
Publisher: Scholastic, Inc.

266
Artist: KEN JOUDREY
Art Director: Peter Schaeffer
Client: International Polygonics Ltd.

267
Artist: WENDY K. POPP
Art Director: Michael Mendelsohn
Publisher: The Franklin Library

268
Artist: WENDELL MINOR
Art Director: Sara Eisenman
Publisher: Alfred A. Knopf, Inc.

269
Artist: TOM NIKOSEY
Art Director: Richard Lebenson / Kathleen Creighton
Publisher: RSVP: The Directory of Creative Talent

270
Artist: SUSAN GRAY

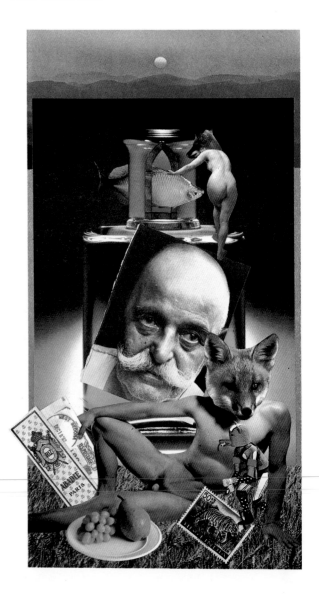

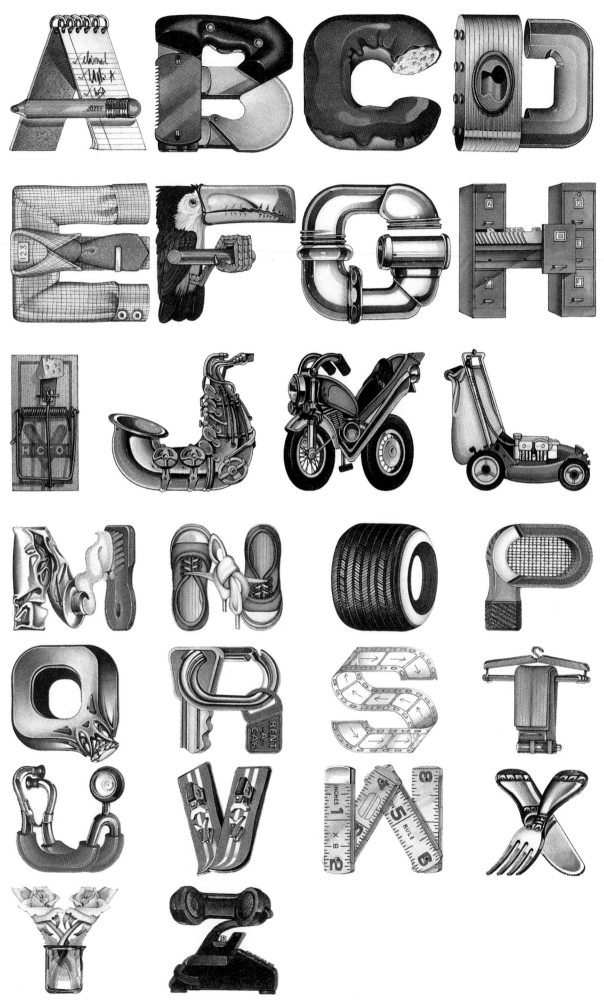

Artist: JÖZEF SUMICHRAST   Art Director: Tim Honnell   Client: Mountain Bell

272
Artist: JUDY PEDERSEN   Art Director: Andrew Kner   Client: RC Publisher

277
Artist: NEIL WALDMAN
Art Director: Steve Edelstein
Client: Government of Grenada

278
Artist: JACQUELINE JASPER

279
Artist: HEIDE OBERHEIDE
Art Director: Laura Glazer
Publisher: Bantam Books

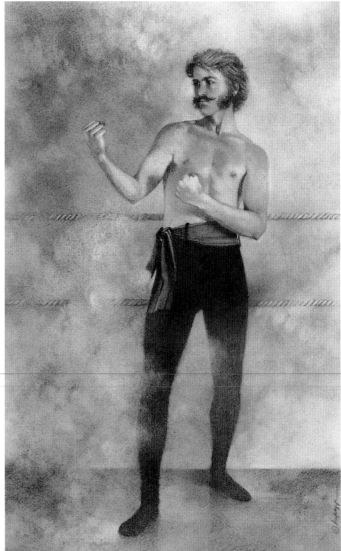

280
Artist: WENDY K. POPP
Art Director: Michael Mendelsohn
Publisher: The Franklin Library

281
Artist: MARK ENGLISH   Art Director: Tim Trabon   Client: Trabon Printing

282
Artist: MICHAEL GARLAND
Art Director: Sylvia Frezzolini
Publisher: William Morrow Junior Books

283
Artist: MICHAEL GARLAND
Art Director: Jean Karl
Publisher: ·Atheneum

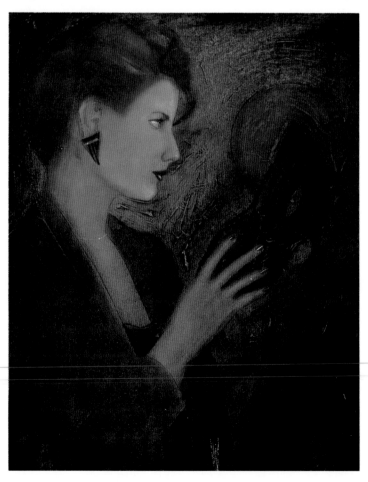

284
Artist: DEBORAH HEALY

285
Artist: ROBERT RODRIGUEZ
Art Director: Roger Carpenter
Publisher: Galliard Press

286
Artist: CHARLES REID
Art Director: Michael Mendelsohn
Publisher: The Franklin Library

288
Artist: BOB CROFUT
Art Director: Michael Mendelsohn
Publisher: The Franklin Library

289
Artist: BOB CROFUT

287
Artist: C. MICHAEL DUDASH
Art Director: Michael Mendelsohn
Publisher: The Franklin Library

Artist: JOHN COLLIER
Art Director: Rita Marshall
Publisher: Creative Education, Inc.

Artist: JOHN M. THOMPSON
Art Director: Marion Davis
Publisher: Reader's Digest

291

Artist: JOHN COLLIER   Art Director: Dale Pollekoff   Publisher: Time-Life Books

293
Artist: MARSHALL ARISMAN
Art Director: Dale Pollekoff / Louis Klein
Publisher: Time-Life Books

294
Artist: MARSHALL ARISMAN
Art Director: Dale Pollekoff / Louis Klein
Publisher: Time-Life Books

295
Artist: STEPHEN ALCORN
Art Director: R.D. Scudellari
Publisher: Modern Library / Random House

296
Artist: STEPHEN ALCORN
Art Director: R.D. Scudellari
Publisher: Modern Library / Random House

297
Artist: STEPHEN ALCORN   Art Director: Sara Eisenman   Publisher: Alfred A. Knopf, Inc.

298

Artist: DAGMAR FRINTA
Art Director: Michael Mendelsohn
Publisher: The Franklin Library

299

Artist: DAGMAR FRINTA
Art Director: Michael Mendelsohn
Publisher: The Franklin Library

300

Artist: KATHERINE MAHONEY
Art Director: Char Lappan
Publisher: Little, Brown & Company

301

Artist: DAVID TAMURA   Art Director: Louise Noble   Publisher: Houghton Mifflin

302

302
Artist: MILTON GLASER   Art Director: Milton Glaser   Publisher: Éditions André Sauret

303
Artist: MILTON GLASER
Art Director: Milton Glaser
Publisher: Éditions André Sauret

304
Artist: MILTON GLASER
Art Director: Milton Glaser
Publisher: Éditions André Sauret

305
Artist: ROBERT QUACKENBUSH
Art Director: Richard Berenson
Publisher: Reader's Digest

306
Artist: BILL RUSSELL
Art Director: Michael Mendelsohn
Publisher: The Franklin Library

307
Artist: JAMES HARVEY WILSON

308
Artist: STAN HUNTER
Art Director: William Gregory
Publisher: Reader's Digest

309
Artist: STAN HUNTER
Art Director: William Gregory
Publisher: Reader's Digest

310
Artist: GUY BILLOUT
Art Director: Louise Fili
Publisher: Pantheon Books

311
Artist: STEVEN GUARNACCIA
Art Director: Joseph Montebello
Publisher: Harper & Row

312
Artist: STEVEN GUARNACCIA
Art Director: Joseph Montebello
Publisher: Harper & Row

Artist: LONNI SUE JOHNSON   Art Director: Louise Fili   Publisher: Pantheon Books

Artist: NANCY STAHL   Art Director: Wendy Boss   Publisher: Villard Books

315
Artist: NICHOLAS GAETANO
Art Director: Judith Loeser
Publisher: Vintage Books

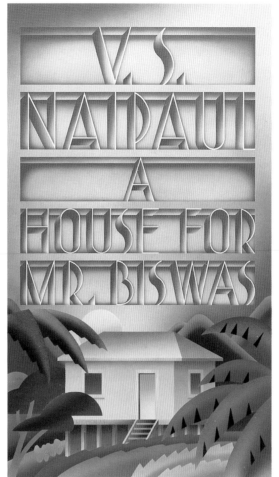

316
Artist: NICHOLAS GAETANO
Art Director: Judith Loeser
Publisher: Vintage Books

317
Artist: NICHOLAS GAETANO
Art Director: Judith Loeser
Publisher: Vintage Books

318
Artist: JUDY PEDERSEN
Art Director: Andrew Kner
Publisher: RC Publications

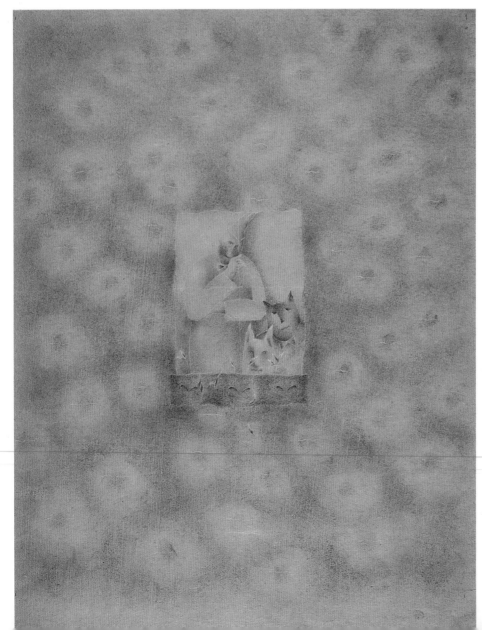

319
Artist: LARK CARRIER

320

Artist: RICHARD SPARKS   Art Director: Angelo Perrone   Publisher: Reader's Digest

Artist: BERNIE FUCHS   Art Director: Marion Davis   Publisher: Reader's Digest

323
Artist: BERNIE FUCHS
Art Director: Marion Davis
Publisher: Readers' Digest

322
Artist: BOB CROFUT
Art Director: Michael Mendelsohn
Publisher: The Franklin Library

324
Artist: MING XIAN CHEN

325
Artist: MING XIAN CHEN

326
Artist: NORMA COWDRICK

327
Artist: NORMA COWDRICK

328
Artist: KEN JOUDREY
Art Director: Dale Fiorillo
Publisher: Dell Publishing

329
Artist: ROBERT McGINNIS
Art Director: Robert McGinnis
Client: Husberg Galleries

330

Artist: LARRY McENTIRE / PATTI J. BISHOP   Art Director: Larry McEntire / Susan Sands   Publisher: Texas Monthly Press

331
Artist: RAFAL OLBINSKI
Art Director: Sara Eisenman
Publisher: Alfred A. Knopf, Inc.

332
Artist: KAREN FARYNIAK   Art Director: Karen Faryniak   Client: Ideas, Inc.

333
Artist: KAREN FARYNIAK
Art Director: Karen Faryniak
Client: Ideas, Inc.

334
Artist: MICHAEL GARLAND

335
Artist: JOHN D. DAWSON
Art Director: Evelyn Bauer
Publisher: Reader's Digest

Artist: JOHN D. DAWSON   Art Director: Evelyn Bauer   Publisher: Reader's Digest

Artist: JOHN D. DAWSON
Art Director: Evelyn Bauer
Publisher: Reader's Digest

338
Artist: MICKEY PARASKEVAS

339
Artist: SUSI KILGORE

340
Artist: MICKEY PARASKEVAS   Art Director: Mickey Paraskevas   Client: Ian Carson

341
Artist: CHRIS BLOSSOM   Art Director: Matt Tepper   Publisher: Avon Books

Artist: MALCOLM T. LIEPKE   Art Director: Angelo Perrone   Publisher: Reader's Digest

343
Artist: MALCOLM T. LIEPKE

344
Artist: MALCOLM T. LIEPKE

345
Artist: CHRIS VAN ALLSBURG
Art Director: Susan M. Sherman
Publisher: Houghton Mifflin

346
Artist: STAN WATTS
Art Director: Stan Watts
Publisher: Galliard Press

347

Artist: KINUKO CRAFT
Art Director: Dale Pollekoff / Louis Klein
Publisher: Time-Life Books

348

Artist: JOHN JUDE PALENCAR
Art Director: Dale Pollekoff / Louis Klein
Publisher: Time-Life Books

349

Artist: JOHN JUDE PALENCAR
Art Director: Dale Pollekoff / Louis Klein
Publisher: Time-Life Books

350
Artist: SUSAN WALP   Art Director: Louise Fili   Publisher: Pantheon Books

352
Artist: BARRY E. JACKSON
Art Director: Craig Butler
Publisher: The Workbook

351
Artist: DAVE CALVER
Art Director: Louise Fili
Publisher: Pantheon Books

Artist: SUSAN WALP   Art Director: Sara Eisenman   Publisher: Alfred A. Knopf, Inc.

Artist: TOM HALL
Art Director: William Gregory
Publisher: Reader's Digest

Artist: TED LEWIN   Art Director: Carol Goldenberg   Publisher: Clarion Books

356
Artist: CHARLES REID
Art Director: Michael Mendelsohn
Publisher: The Franklin Library

357
Artist: EDWARD SOREL   Art Director: Murray Belsky   Publisher: American Heritage

JURY

JERRY PINKNEY
Chairman
Illustrator

JERRY ALLISON
Illustrator

JOHN BERG
Art Director, V.P.,
CBS Records

MICHAEL DAVID BROWN
Illustrator

ALAN E. COBER
Illustrator

JUDY GARLAN
Art Director,
The Atlantic Monthly

STANLEY MELTZOFF
Illustrator

ROBERT PLISKIN
Creative Head, President,
The First Team, Inc.

TERESA WOODWARD
Illustrator

AWARD WINNERS

BILL MAYER
Gold Medal

TERESA FASOLINO
Silver Medal

DANIEL MAFFIA
Silver Medal

EDWARD SOREL
Gold Medal

MARSHALL ARISMAN
Silver Medal

ADVERTISING

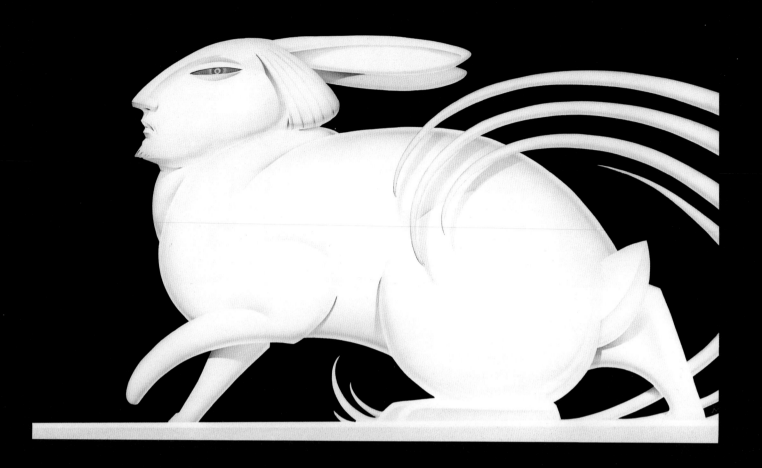

359
Artist: BILL MAYER
Art Director: Brad Copeland
Agency: Cooper-Copeland
Client: William Acree Company

GOLD MEDAL

361

Artist: MARSHALL ARISMAN
Art Director: Susan Belviso
Client: Tidewater Society of Communicating Arts

SILVER MEDAL

362
Artist: TERESA FASOLINO
Art Director: Milton Glaser
Client: Grand Union Supermarkets

SILVER MEDAL

363
Artist: EMANUAL SCHONGOT
Art Director: Joseph Stelmach
Client: RCA Records

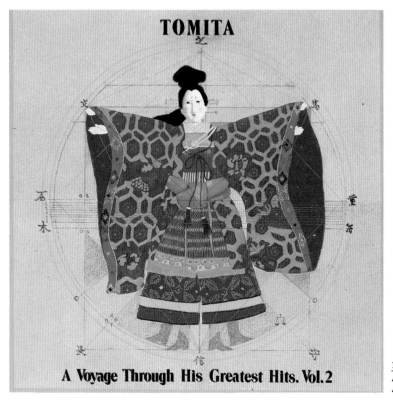

364
Artist: STEPHANIE A. ENGLISH
Art Director: John Collier

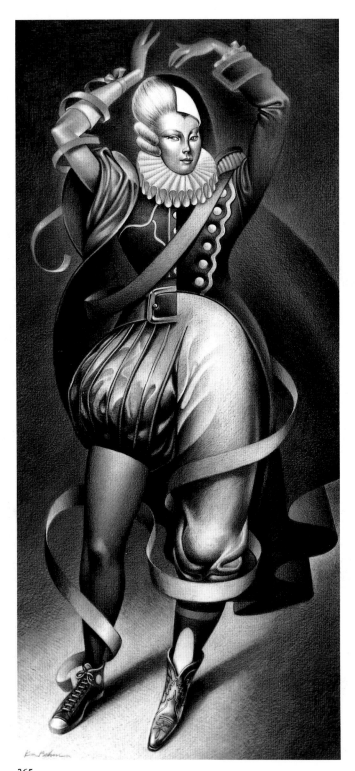

365
Artist: KIM BEHM
Art Director: Hank Knerr
Client: University of Northern Iowa

366
Artist: MEL ODOM
Art Director: Heather Bartling
Agency: William, Douglas, McAdams
Client: Wyeth Laboratories

367
Artist: MICKEY PARASKEVAS

368

Artist: FRED OTNES   Art Director: Stephanie Lucas   Client: American Microsystems, Inc.

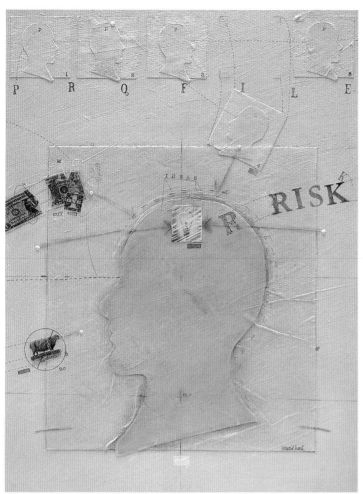

369
Artist: DAVID LESH
Art Director: Mark Ulrich
Client: American Telephone & Telegraph

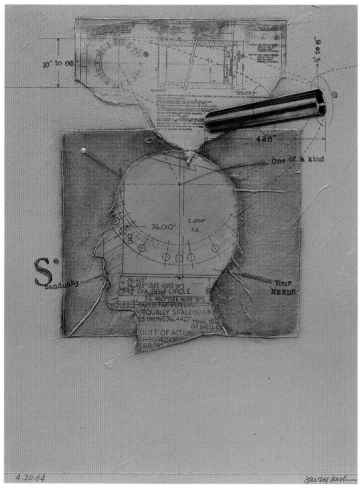

370
Artist: DAVID LESH
Art Director: Kathy Rennels
Agency: Fahlgren & Swink
Client: Sandusky Foundry

371
Artist: JOHN A. WILSON
Art Director: Michael Labiak
Agency: Ross Roy, Inc.
Client: Chrysler Corporation

372
Artist: ROBERT A. OLSON
Art Director: Len Mitsch
Agency: Clarke, Livingston
Client: Westlaw

373
Artist: JEFF PIENKOS

374
Artist: CURT DOTY
Art Director: David Mocarski
Client: Metropolitan Museum of Art

375
Artist: SANDY HUFFAKER
Art Director: Sandy Huffaker / Ron Meyerson
Client: Newsweek

376
Artist: BILL MAYER
Art Director: Dennis Hagen
Agency: Bozell & Jacobs
Client: Illinois Lottery

377
Artist: GERRY GERSTEN
Art Director: Tim Hamill
Agency: Bernstein-Rein
Client: United Telecom

378
Artist: GERRY GERSTEN
Art Director: Yuriko Gamo
Agency: Lord, Geller, Federico, Einstein
Client: Quality Paperback

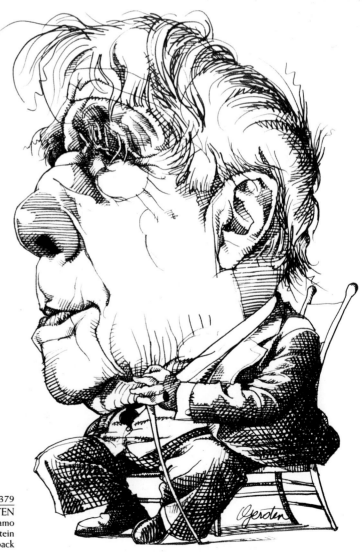

379
Artist: GERRY GERSTEN
Art Director: Yuriko Gamo
Agency: Lord, Geller, Federico, Einstein
Client: Quality Paperback

380
Artist: WILSON McLEAN
Art Director: Dick Loomis
Agency: The Paige Group
Client: Mohawk Paper Mills, Inc.

381
Artist: ARTHUR LIDOV

382
Artist: BARRON STOREY
Art Director: Robin Knowlton
Client: San Francisco Mime Troop

383
Artist: STEFF GEISSBUHLER
Art Director: Steff Geissbuhler
Client: Alvin Ailey American Dance Theatre

384
Artist: IVAN CHERMAYEFF
Art Director: Ivan Chermayeff
Client: Jacob's Pillow

385
Artist: SANTO PEZZUTTI
Art Director: Santo Pezzutti
Client: Monmouth Arts Council

386
Artist: EDWARD SOREL
Art Director: Bennett Robinson
Client: Mead Paper

387

Artist: CAROL WALD   Art Director: Mary Macenka   Client: Seattle Symphony

388
Artist: CAROL WALD
Art Director: Victor Weaver / Jerry Counihan
Client: Dell Publishing

389
Artist: JEAN-FRANCOIS PODEVIN
Art Director: Jean-Francois Podevin / Debra Jean Rawdin
Client: Steve Roach

Artist: **GARY KELLEY**   Art Director: **Jim Borcherdt**   Agency: **D'Arcy McManus & Masius**   Client: **Michelob**

391
Artist: JUDY CLIFFORD   Art Director: Jessica Weber   Client: Book-of-the-Month Club

392
Artist: MARK CHICKINELLI
Art Director: Bill Barder
Client: Hellman Associates

393
Artist: EDWARD ABRAMS
Art Director: Marvin Schwartz
Client: Angel Records

Imagine your child with nothing to imagine.

394
Artist: TOMIE DE PAOLA
Art Director: Bill Zabowski
Agency: Martin / Williams
Client: Children's Theatre Company

395
Artist: PATTY DRYDEN
Art Director: Mark Larson
Client: CBS Records

396
Artist: DAVID LESH   Art Director: Dawn Keller / John Nagy   Agency: Caldwell, Van Riper   Client: Blue Cross

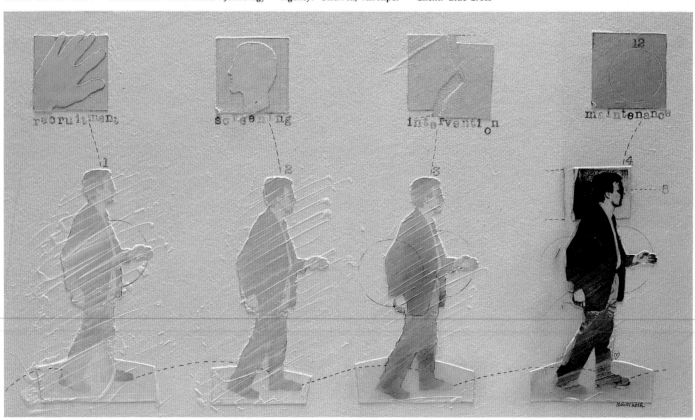

397
Artist: NURIT BOCHNER
Art Director: Carol Marunas
Client: Leningrad Symphony Orchestra

398

Artist: **GARY KELLEY**   Art Director: Gary Kelley   Client: Dallas Illustrators

399
Artist: ELLEN RIXFORD
Art Director: John Fraioli
Agency: Bergelt Advertising
Client: PPF

400
Artist: GLENN HARRINGTON
Art Director: Arlan Ettinger
Agency: Ettinger Advertising
Client: Morton Bernard

401
Artist: STAN WATTS
Art Director: Stan Watts
Client: MCA Records

402
Artist: STAN WATTS
Art Director: Stan Watts / Murry Whiteman
Client: Polygram Records

403

Artist: BILL MAYER
Art Director: Harris Milligan
Client: Harris Milligan

404

Artist: EZRA N. TUCKER
Art Director: Nancy Donald / Tony Lane
Client: CBS Records

405
Artist: TOM CURRY
Art Director: Mike Mentler
Client: Anheuser Busch

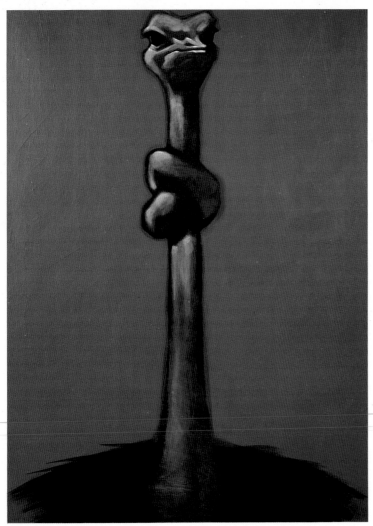

406
Artist: CURT DOTY
Art Director: Philip Hays
Client: World Hunger Project

407
Artist: RAFAL OLBINSKI   Art Director: Debbie Johnson   Agency: J. Walter Thompson Company   Client: Deawoo Corporation

408

Artist: CATHLEEN TOELKE
Art Director: Jamie Mambro
Agency: Welch, Currier, Smith, Inc.
Client: Rand Typography

409
Artist: RICHARD WEHRMAN
Art Director: Mike Fountain
Agency: Rumrill Hoyte
Client: Remington

410
Artist: BRALDT BRALDS   Art Director: Norman Egelston   Agency: The Agency   Client: Barclay's Bank

411
Artist: JIM CARSON
Art Director: Margery Stegman
Client: Graphic Artists Guild

412: SEYMOUR CHWAST   Art Director: John W. Channell   Client: Sony Corporation of America

413
Artist: SEYMOUR CHWAST   Art Director: John W. Channell   Client: Sony Corporation of America

414
Artist: MILTON GLASER   Art Director: Joe LaRosa   Agency: Waring & LaRosa, Inc.   Client: Perrier

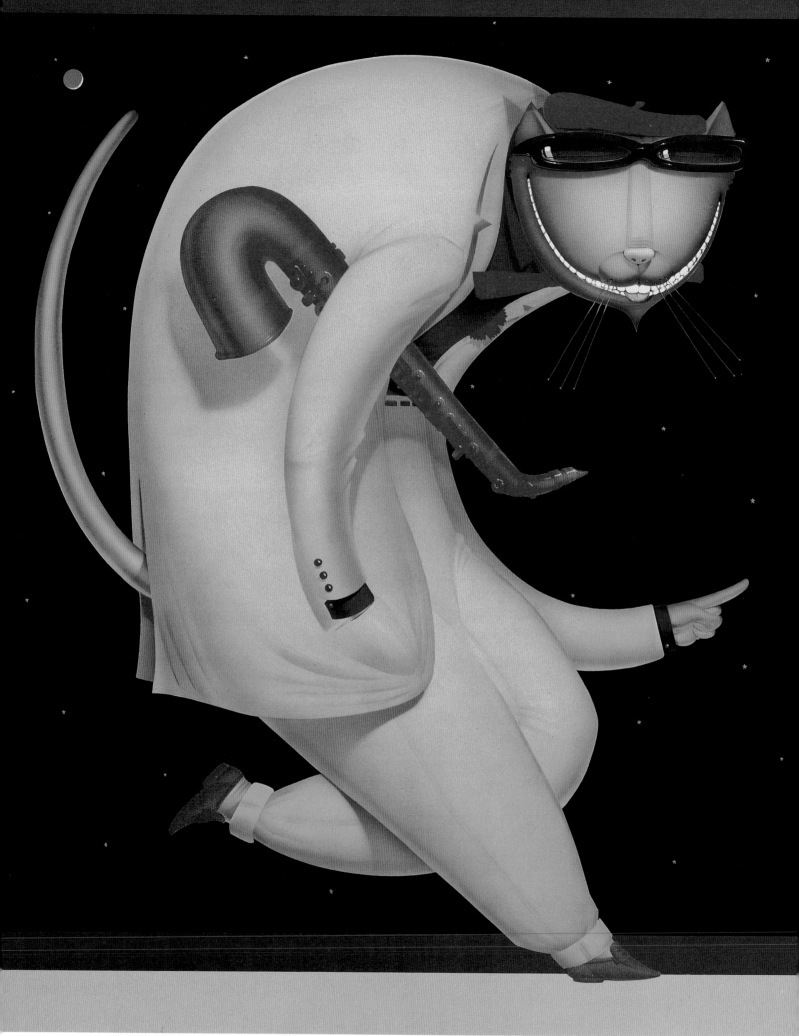

415

Artist: BILL MAYER   Art Director: Bill Mayer / Doug Vachion   Client: Atlanta Jazz Festival

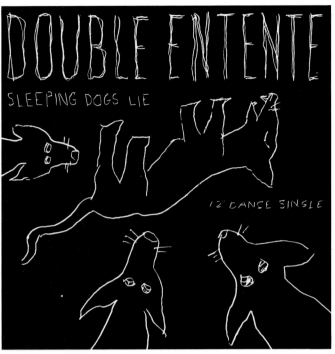

416
Artist: TONY LANE
Art Director: Tony Lane / Nancy Donald
Client: CBS Records

417
Artist: LANE SMITH
Art Director: Lane Smith
Client: PVC Records

418
Artist: MATTHEW IMPERIALE   Art Director: Bruce Crocker   Agency: Altman & Manley Advertising   Client: Sweet Micro Systems

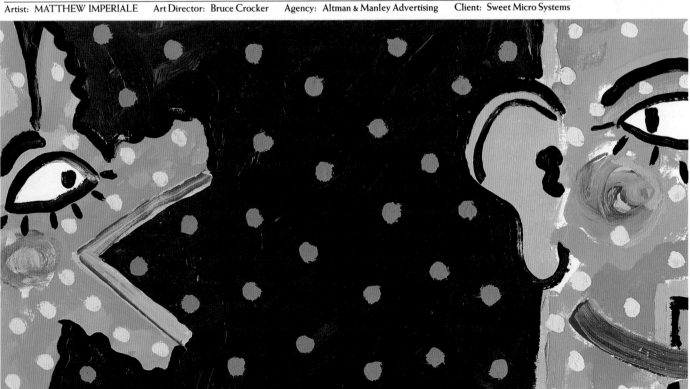

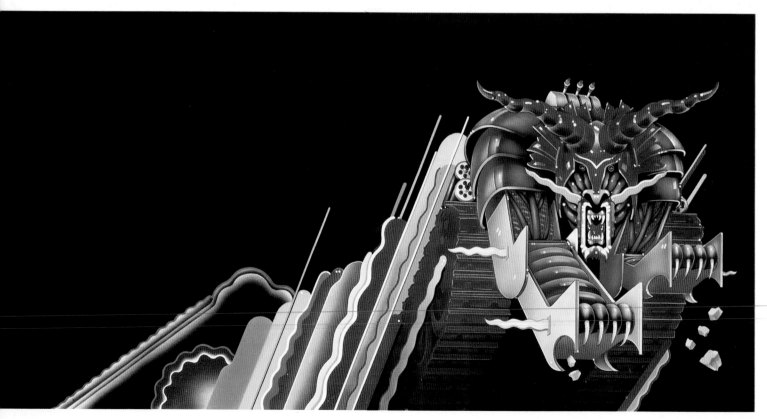

421

Artist: ROBERT HEINDEL   **Art Director:** Gery Freidland   **Agency:** Benton & Bowles, Inc.   **Client:** Caltex

Artist: PAUL DAVIS   Art Director: Paul Davis   Client: Big Apple Circus

423
Artist: TOM CURRY
Art Director: Donna Kolis
Agency: Rives, Smith, Baldwin & Carlberg
Client: First City Savings

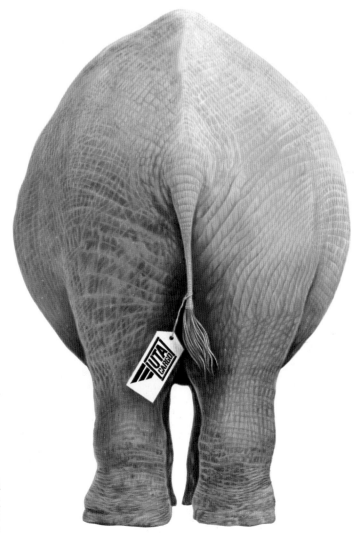

424
Artist: DENNIS CARMICHAEL
Art Director: Wes Keebler
Agency: Cunningham & Walsh
Client: U.T.A. Airlines

425
Artist: THOMAS BLACKSHEAR II
Art Director: Mike Murata
Agency: Medlin & Associates
Client: Proton

426
Artist: JEROME COUDRAY
Art Director: Tony Lane / Nancy Donald
Client: CBS Records

Artist: ED SOYKA   Art Director: Dick Davis   Agency: Altman & Manley Advertising   Client: Jaclar Sneakers

428

Artist: BRALDT BRALDS   Art Director: Bob Barrie   Agency: Falcon, McElligott & Rice   Client: Minnesota Zoo

Artist: MARK ENGLISH   Art Director: Bill Erlacher   Client: Artists Associates

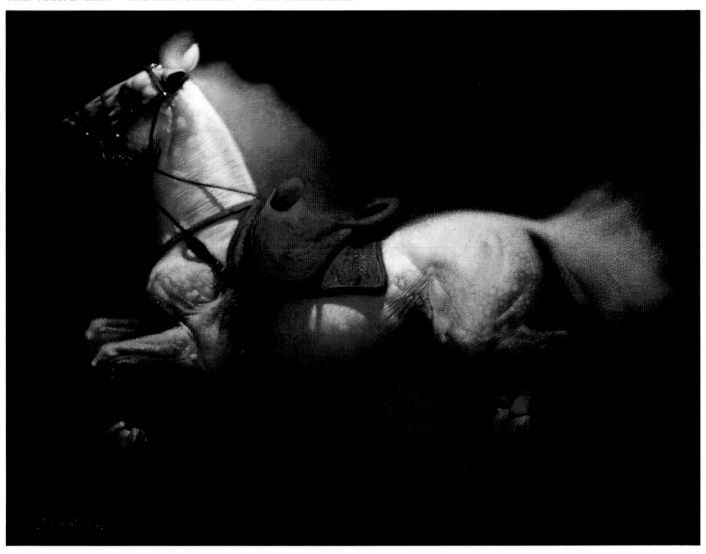

430

Artist: CHARLES KATINAS   Art Director: Karen Kutner Katinas   Client: International Paper Company

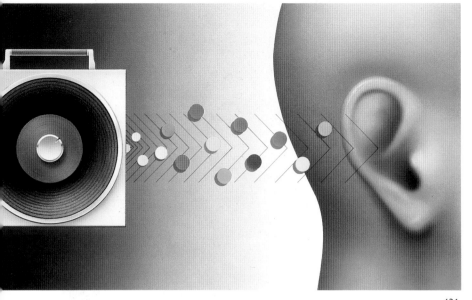

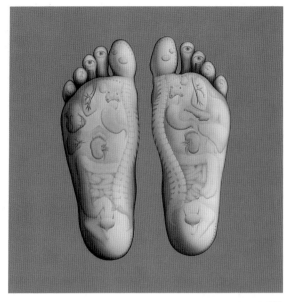

431
Artist: STANISLAW FERNANDES
Art Director: Jerry Laufman
Client: Sony Corporation of America

432
Artist: LEONARD E. MORGAN
Art Director: Michael V. Phillips
Agency: Frank J. Corbett, Inc.
Client: Westwood Pharmaceuticals

433
Artist: IVAN CHERMAYEFF
Art Director: Ivan Chermayeff
Client: Mobil Oil Corporation

434

Artist: ALEX EBEL   Art Director: Les Kerr   Agency: Ackerman & McQueen   Client: Nocona Boot Company

435

Artist: DAVID LUI   Art Director: Esther Liu   Client: Asian Cine Vision, Inc.

436

Artist: LESLIE ROBIN
Art Director: Joe Chlumsky
Agency: Deere & Company Advertising
Client: Deere & Company

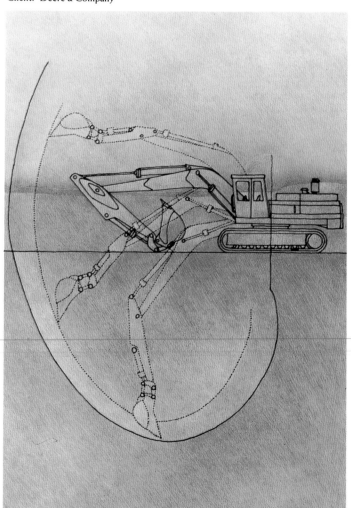

437

Artist: CATHY BARANCIK
Art Director: Susan Herridge
Client: Minneapolis Star & Tribune

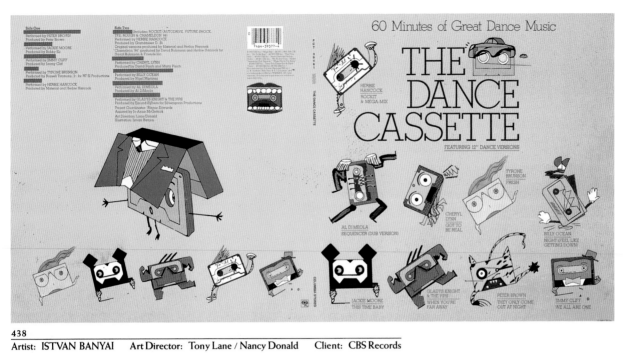

438

Artist: ISTVAN BANYAI   Art Director: Tony Lane / Nancy Donald   Client: CBS Records

439

Artist: NANCY STAHL   Art Director: Christopher Austopchuk   Client: CBS Records

441
Artist: STEPHEN SAWYER
Art Director: Stephen Sawyer
Client: Master Graphics

440
Artist: THEO RUDNAK
Art Director: Elaine Catanzarite
Agency: Group 2 Atlanta
Client: Novatel

442
Artist: ROBERT WISNER
Art Director: Robert Wisner
Agency: Hutchins / Y&R
Client: Rochester Sesquicentennial Committee

443
Artist: THEO RUDNAK
Art Director: Elaine Catanzarite
Agency: Group 2 Atlanta
Client: Novatel

Artist: VIVIENNE FLESHER
Art Director: Barbara Loveland
Client: Herman Miller Corporation

Artist: BARBARA NESSIM
Art Director: Barbara Loveland
Client: Herman Miller Corporation

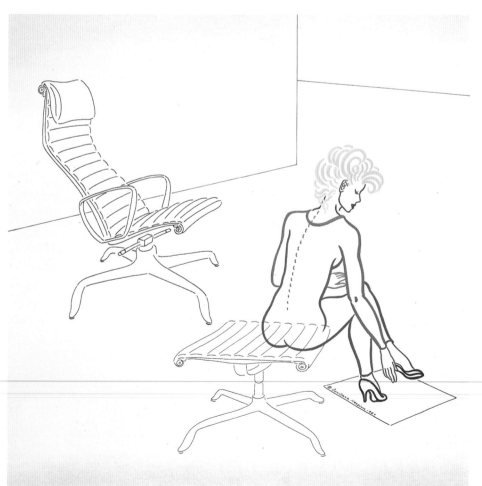

446
Artist: JOHN COLLIER
Art Director: Howard Title
Agency: Waring & LaRosa, Inc.
Client: Grand Specialties, Inc.

447
Artist: RAFAL OLBINSKI
Art Director: Ron Kellum
Client: RCA Records

448
Artist: FRED OTNES   Art Director: Carla Bauer   Client: E.F. Hutton

449
Artist: FRED OTNES
Client: Artists Associates

450

Artist: FRED OTNES   Art Director: Carla Bauer   Client: E.F. Hutton

451

Artist: ABDUL MATI KLARWEIN
Art Director: Tony Lane / Nancy Donald
Client: CBS Records

Ivan Chermayeff: Works and Process
April 27 - June 17 1984
The Addison Gallery
of American Art.
Phillips Academy
Andover, Mass.

Artist: IVAN CHERMAYEFF   Art Director: Ivan Chermayeff   Client: Addison Gallery of American Art

453
Artist: JEFF LARAMORE
Art Director: Jeff Laramore
Agency: Young & Laramore
Client: Shorewood Corporation

454
Artist: ANNE M. GILMARTIN
Art Director: Anne M. Gilmartin
Client: Carson-Gilmartin Travel, Inc.

455
Artist: NANCY FREEMAN

456
Artist: BRAD HOLLAND   Art Director: Mario Jamora   Agency: Dorritie & Lyons   Client: Abbott Laboratories

457
Artist: GARY MEYER
Art Director: Rick Albert
Client: Film Ventures International

458
Artist: MARK PENBERTHY
Art Director: Judy Dimon / Mark Penberthy
Client: Shearson, Lehman / American Express

459
Artist: BART GOLDMAN   Art Director: Don Weller   Client: Alpha Graphix

460

Artist: WILLIAM LOW   Art Director: Ellen Suekier / Andrew Kner   Client: The New York Times

461
Artist: JOAN STEINER   Art Director: Emil Micha   Client: The New York Times

462
Artist: SCOTT REYNOLDS
Art Director: Jeffrey Leder
Client: The Barrick Group, Inc.

463
Artist: VIVIENNE FLESHER
Art Director: Ellen Kier
Client: The New York Times

464

Artist: PAUL GIOVANOPOULOS   Art Director: Mike Rizzo   Agency: Marsteller, Inc.   Client: Dow Corning

465

Artist: PAUL GIOVANOPOULOS   Art Director: Mike Rizzo   Agency: Marsteller, Inc.   Client: Dow Corning

466
Artist: MARK McMAHON
Art Director: Mary Beth Cybil
Client: Rubloff

467
Artist: SCOTT REYNOLDS
Art Director: Jeffrey Leder
Client: The Barrick Group, Inc.

Artist: STEVEN GUARNACCIA
Art Director: Bob Manley
Agency: Altman & Manley Advertising

Artist: JOAN LANDIS
Art Director: Diane Meier
Agency: Meier Advertising, Inc.
Client: Balducci's

469

Artist: SEYMOUR CHWAST   Art Director: John W. Channell   Client: Sony Corporation of America

471

Artist: LOU MYERS   Art Director: Hans Peter Weiss   Agency: G.G.K.   Client: I.B.M.

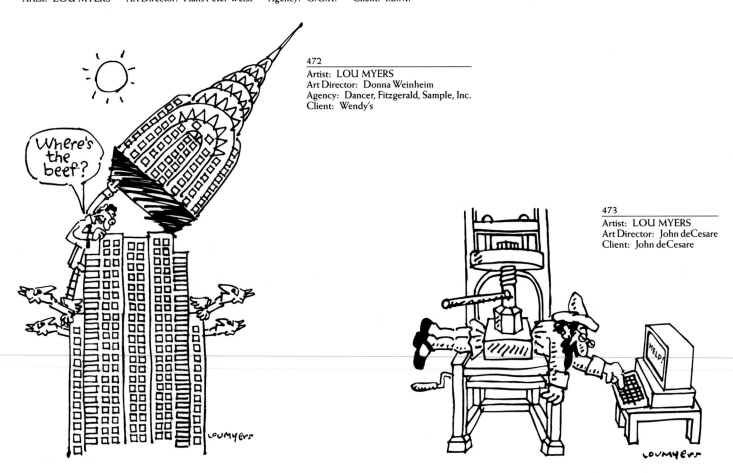

472
Artist: LOU MYERS
Art Director: Donna Weinheim
Agency: Dancer, Fitzgerald, Sample, Inc.
Client: Wendy's

473
Artist: LOU MYERS
Art Director: John deCesare
Client: John deCesare

474
Artist: ED RENFRO
Art Director: John Berg
Client: Columbia Records / CBS

475
Artist: RICK MEYEROWITZ   Art Director: Douglas Grimmett   Client: Workman Publishing Company

476
Artist: CAROL WALD
Art Director: Kathleen Creighton / Stephen Bodkin
Client: RSVP; The Directory of Creative Talent

477
Artist: SUSI KILGORE   Client: Synergistics

478

Artist: ROBERT GUNN   Art Director: Kathryn Sherwood   Agency: Frankenberry / Laughlin & Constable   Client: Wisconsin Electric

479
Artist: ALAN E. COBER   Art Director: David G. Foote   Client: United States Postal Service

480
Artist: BARBARA NESSIM
Art Director: Barbara Soll
Client: New York University

481
Artist: PAUL MEISEL
Art Director: Robert Jensen
Client: Walker Art Center

482
Artist: W.B. PARK
Art Director: Joe Carty
Agency: Impact
Client: Project Software & Development, Inc.

483
Artist: BERNIE FUCHS   Art Director: Gene Federico   Agency: Lord, Geller, Federico, Einstein   Client: Schumacher & Company

484
Artist: ROBERT M. CUNNINGHAM   Art Director: Bennett Robinson   Client: Mead Paper

485

Artist: KAREN FARYNIAK   Art Director: Karen Faryniak   Client: Color Services

JURY

JAMES R. CROWELL
Chairman
Illustrator

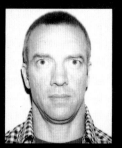

PETER COX
Illustrator

CHARLES KADIN
Director, Graphic Art,
Harlequin Books

DICK KOHFIELD
Illustrator

CHARLES LONG
Art Director,
Evergreen Advertising

GENE MYDLOWSKI
Art Director, Designer,
Photographer

CHARLES SANTORE
Illustrator

CHAS. B. SLACKMAN
Illustrator

MATT TEPPER
Art Director,
Avon Books

AWARD WINNERS

ATTILA HEJJA
Gold Medal

BOB PEAK
Gold Medal

JAMES E. TENNISON
Gold Medal

THOMAS KITTS
Silver Medal

GLENN HARRINGTON
Silver Medal

GARY KELLEY
Silver Medal

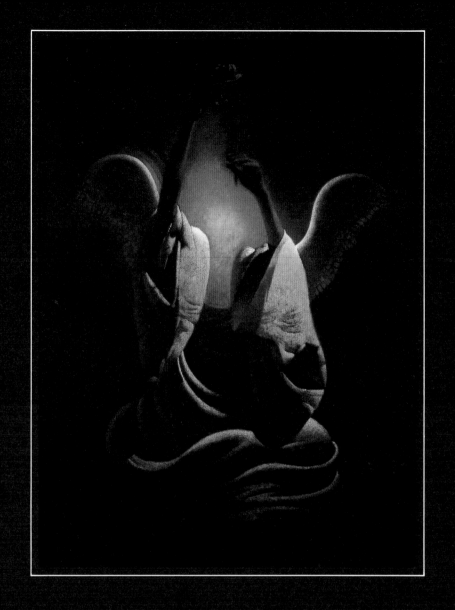

INSTITUTIONAL

486
Artist: ATTILA HEJJA
Art Director: Robert Schulman
Client: National Aeronautics & Space Administration

GOLD MEDAL   HAMILTON KING AWARD

489
Artist: THOMAS KITTS
Art Director: Robert Bailey
Client: American Institute Of Architects

SILVER MEDAL

491

Artist: GLENN HARRINGTON
Art Director: Glenn Harrington
Client: Barbara Gordon Associates

SILVER MEDAL

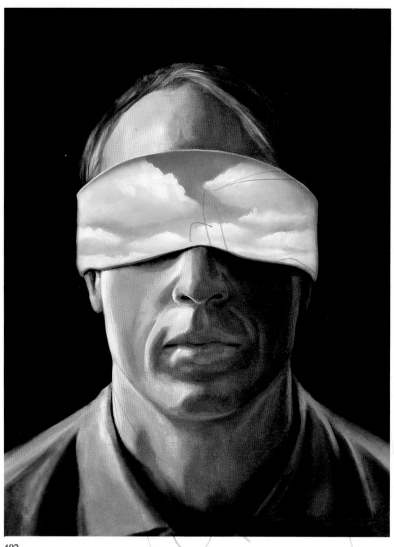

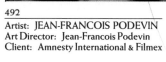

492
Artist: JEAN-FRANCOIS PODEVIN
Art Director: Jean-Francois Podevin
Client: Amnesty International & Filmex

493
Artist: JIM GALLAGHER
Art Director: Jim Gallagher

494
Artist: DARRYL ZUDECK   Client: Visual Arts Portfolio Book

495
Artist: DARRYL ZUDECK   Client: Visual Arts Portfolio Book

Artist: KEN PARKHURST   Art Director: Gerry Rosentswieg   Client: California State Museum of Science & Industry

497
Artist: ROBERT A. OLSON
Art Director: Len Mitsch
Agency: Clarke, Livingston
Client: Westlaw

498
Artist: MALCOLM T. LIEPKE
Art Director: Jerry Lawrence
Agency: Wunderman, Ricotta & Kline
Client: Aim Marketing

499
Artist: PAUL DAVIS
Art Director: Paul Davis
Client: Greater New York Conference On Soviet Jewry

500
Artist: MILTON GLASER
Art Director: Milton Glaser
Client: Zanders Feinpapiere

501
Artist: MILTON GLASER
Art Director: Milton Glaser
Client: Zanders Feinpapiere

502
Artist: STEVE KARCHIN
Art Director: John Dzmil
Agency: Bozell & Jacobs
Client: American Telephone & Telegraph

503
Artist: HOWARD KOSLOW
Art Director: James Helzer
Client: Fleetwood

504
Artist: HOWARD KOSLOW
Art Director: James Helzer
Client: Fleetwood

506
Artist: BARRON STOREY
Art Director: Jerry McDaniel
Client: Society Of Illustrators

505
Artist: JEFFREY SMITH
Art Director: Roger Black
Client: American Institute Of Graphic Arts

507
Artist: STEVEN GUARNACCIA   Art Director: Steven Guarnaccia   Client: Scarlett Letters

Artist: BILL FINEWOOD   Art Director: Linda Orman   Client: Corn Hill Neighbors

510
Artist: NANCY LAWTON
Art Director: Bennett Robinson
Client: H.J. Heinz Company

512
Artist: DICK LUBEY
Art Director: Ron Ketchum
Client: Park Avenue Pub

513
Artist: JAMES E. TENNISON
Art Director: Scott Turner
Agency: Weekley & Associates
Client: Shakespeare In The Park, Fort Worth, Texas

514
Artist: GREG SPALENKA

515
Artist: MATT MAHURIN

516
Artist: LESLIE WU

517
Artist: ANN MEISEL
Art Director: Robert M. Fitch
Client: Paper Moon Graphics

518
Artist: FRANK RICCIO

519
Artist: IZUMI INOUE

520
Artist: PAMELA HIGGINS PATRICK
Art Director: Pamela Higgins Patrick
Client: Art Store, Inc.

521

Artist: BILL NELSON   Art Director: Bill Nelson   Client: Theatre IV

522
Artist: DAVID TAYLOR
Art Director: David Taylor
Client: Billy Graham Museum

523
Artist: BOB PEAK   Art Director: David G. Foote   Client: United States Postal Service

Artist: THOMAS BLACKSHEAR II
Art Director: Horace Skeete
Agency: H.S. & B. Advertising
Client: Smirnoff Vodka

525
Artist: THOMAS BLACKSHEAR II
Art Director: Horace Skeete
Agency: H.S. & B. Advertising
Client: Smirnoff Vodka

526
Artist: THOMAS BLACKSHEAR II

527
Artist: HEATHER COOPER
Client: Cigna Corporation

528
Artist: BART FORBES
Art Director: Jack Summerford
Client: Harvey Paper Company

Artist: PAUL DAVIS   Art Director: Paul Davis   Agency: Davis & Russek   Client: Theaterworks / U.S.A.

530
Artist: TED COCONIS

531
Artist: KIMANNE UHLER
Art Director: Patricia Watkins
Client: Burroughs Welcome Company

532
Artist: ROBERT HUNT
Art Director: Robert Hunt
Client: San Francisco Society Of Illustrators Auction

533
Artist: DAVID RANKIN

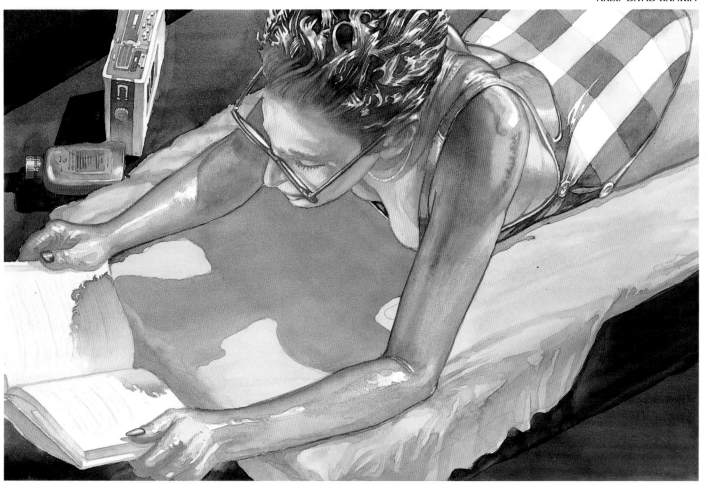

534

Artist: WILSON McLEAN   Art Director: Wilson McLean   Client: Roger Sobell

535
Artist: RICHARD SPARKS   Art Director: Richard Sparks   Client: Save The Children

536
Artist: BOB CONGE
Art Director: Barbara Brecher
Client: United States Surgeon General / University Of Rochester Medical Center

537
Artist: JEFF CORNELL
Art Director: Joe Loya
Client: Save The Children

538
Artist: GARY KELLEY
Art Director: Gary Kelley
Client: Art Directors Club Of Cincinnati

539
Artist: PAUL ORLANDO
Art Director: Kathy Fulton
Client: Maritz, Inc.

540
Artist: G. ALLEN GARNS
Art Director: Kent Looft
Client: Graphic Process

541
Artist: GREG MORAES

542
Artist: DAVID SHANNON
Art Director: Jerry Seally
Client: Cleveland Plain Dealer

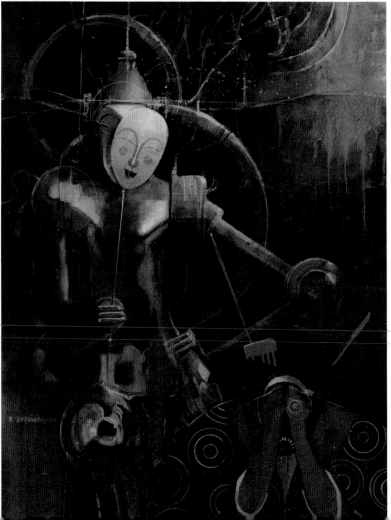

543
Artist: BILL SIENKIEWICZ
Art Director: Robert Baxter

544
Artist: BIRNEY LETTICK   Art Director: Kathleen Creighton / Stephen Bodkin   Client: RSVP; The Directory Of Creative Talent

545
Artist: DICK LUBEY

Pumpkin Chip Cookies

1 C. plus 2 T. sifted flour	1/2 C. soft butter
1/2 tsp. baking soda	1/2 C. chopped walnuts
1/2 tsp. salt	1 pkg. (6oz.) semisweet
1/2 C. granulated sugar	chocolate pieces
3/4 C. dark-brown sugar	1 tsp. cinnamon
firmly packed	1/2 tsp. nutmeg
1 egg	1/4 tsp. ground cloves
1/2 C. pumpkin	1/4 tsp. ginger

1. Preheat oven to 375 F.
2. Sift flour with soda, salt, & spices into bowl.
3. Beat sugars and butter together using mixer. Add egg and pumpkin, beat.
4. Add dry ingredients and beat until smooth — about 1 minute.
5. Stir in nuts and chocolate chips.
6. Drop by teaspoonfuls, 2 inches apart, onto un- greased cookie sheet.
7. Bake 10 to 12 minutes. Remove to wire rack; cool.

Makes about 3 Dozen Cookies

547
Artist: MICHAEL PATRICK CRONAN
Art Director: Michael Patrick Cronan
Client: Farmers' Savings Bank

548
Artist: GARRY NICHOLS

549
Artist: ROBERT A. OLSON
Art Director: Robert A. Olson
Client: Windemere Galleries

550
Artist: ERIC VELASQUEZ

551
Artist: GEORGE GUZZI

552
Artist: PAT SOPER

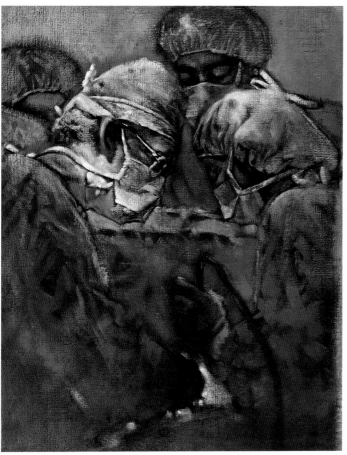

553
Artist: RICHARD SPARKS
Art Director: Peter Nuhn
Client: Yale-New Haven Hospital

554
Artist: DAVID ELLIOTT
Art Director: Joe Morin
Agency: Morin Advertising
Client: Morin Advertising Art

555
Artist: PETER McCAFFREY   **Art Director:** Peter McCaffrey   **Client:** Yo-Chester Of Rochester Inc.

556
Artist: BILL SIENKIEWICZ   Art Director: Robert Baxter

557
Artist: CAROLE KABRIN   Art Director: Jack Fleshig   Client: WXYZ-TV

558
Artist: GEORGE FERNANDEZ

559
Artist: ROBERT HYNES

560
Artist: REGAN DUNNICK
Art Director: Steven Sessions
Client: The Nashville Network

561
Artist: GIL COHEN   Art Director: Joseph Baumer   Client: United States Information Agency

562
Artist: G. ALLEN GARNS
Client: Leslie Levy Gallery

563
Artist: MICHAEL YOUNG   Client: Tina Millge

564
Artist: LARRY A. GERBER
Client: Halsey Publishers

565
Artist: LARRY A. GERBER   Client: Halsey Publishers

566
Artist: SCOTT GORDLEY   Art Director: Scott Gordley   Client: Network Studios

567
Artist: ROBERT GIUSTI   Art Director: Shinichiro Tora / Mitsutoshi Hosaka   Client: Hotel Barmen's Association

568
Artist: STAN GRANT   Art Director: Judy Slapin   Client: Eastman Publishing

Artist: CARL LUNDGREN   Art Director: Gene Mydlowski   Client: Berkley Books

572
Artist: MARK GRAHAM

573
Artist: FRANK RILEY   Art Director: Marjorie Crane   Client: Electronic Fun Magazine

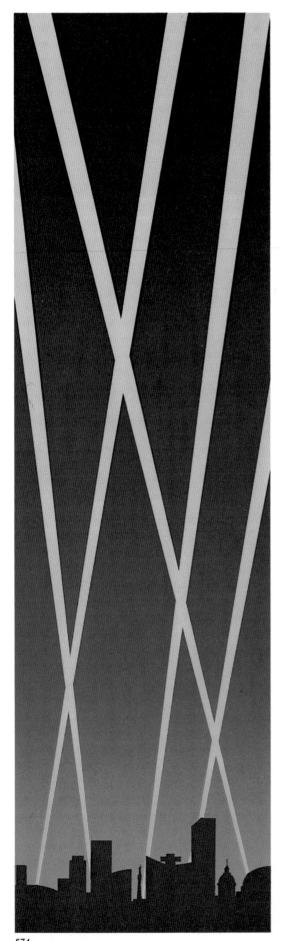

574
Artist: JEFF LARAMORE
Art Director: Jeff Laramore
Agency: Young & Laramore
Client: Porter Foundation

575
Artist: JEFF LARAMORE
Art Director: Jeff Laramore
Agency: Young & Laramore
Client: Indianapolis Symphony Orchestra

576
Artist: KAREN FARYNIAK
Art Director: Karen Faryniak
Client: Ideas, Inc.

577
Artist: CRAIG TENNANT

578
Artist: BURT SILVERMAN
Art Director: Edward Gold
Client: Loyola University

579
Artist: PAUL M. GLEASON
Art Director: Roger Moore
Client: Laguna Pacific Publishing

580

Artist: R. KENTON NELSON   Art Director: R. Kenton Nelson   Client: Norm Reed / Americafest

581

Artist: FRED FREEMAN   Art Director: Nick Kiriloff   Client: National Park Service

582

Artist: ALBERT LORENZ   Art Director: Terry Edelman   Client: Commodity Exchange

583

Artist: WILLIAM V. CIGLIANO   Art Director: Randy Kaden   Agency: Phase II   Client: Canteen Corporatio

584
Artist: ROBERT J. BYRD
Client: Robert J. Byrd

585
Artist: JOYCE A. HAYASHI
Client: Hallmark Cards, Inc.

586
Artist: ROLLAND DINGMAN

587
Artist: ALEX MURAWSKI
Art Director: Robert Qually
Agency: Qually & Company, Inc.
Client: Standard Brands

588
Artist: RODICA PRATO   Client: Rodica Prato

589
Artist: WILSON McLEAN   Art Director: Jack Odet   Client: Citicorp

Artist: ROBERT LO GRIPPO   Art Director: Robert Lo Grippo   Client: American Artists Group

Artist: SANDI S. KING   Art Director: Jan Rice   Client: Hallmark Cards, Inc.

593
Artist: JAMES E. TENNISON
Art Director: John McEown
Agency: Tracy-Locke / BBDO
Client: United States Outdoor Diving Championships

594
Artist: ROBERT HEINDEL
Art Director: Scott Brady
Agency: Muir Cornelius Moore
Client: Champion Paper

592
Artist: G. ALLEN GARNS
Art Director: Anne Hubbard
Client: Phoenix Portfolio

595
Artist: BRYAN HONKAWA
Art Director: Scott A. Mednick / Douglas Boyd
Agency: Douglas Boyd Design & Marketing
Client: Gore Graphics

596
Artist: PETER FIORE   Art Director: Donna Purcell   Agency: Gross Townsend & Frank   Client: Cutter Pharmaceutical

597
Artist: JIM BUCKELS
Art Director: Kelly Weaver
Client: National Balloon Championships

598
Artist: DENNIS LUZAK
Client: Dennis Luzak

599
Artist: MARK BRAUGHT
Client: Mark Braught

600
Artist: BOB PEAK   Art Director: David G. Foote   Client: United States Postal Service

601
Artist: BOB PEAK   Art Director: David G. Foote   Client: United States Postal Service

Artist: MICHAEL DAVID BROWN   Art Director: Michael David Brown   Client: American Telephone & Telegraph

603
Artist: DAVID JEMERSON YOUNG
Art Director: David Jemerson Young
Agency: Young & Laramore
Client: Indianapolis Racquet Clubs

604
Artist: ROBERT HEINDEL
Art Director: David Hicks
Agency: David Hicks Productions
Client: University Of Oklahoma

605
Artist: CLIFF SPOHN
Art Director: Dave Carter / Denise Spaulding
Agency: David E. Carter Corporation
Client: Decathlon Corporation

606
Artist: REGAN DUNNICK
Art Director: Melanie Moskowitz
Agency: Walker, Fuld
Client: American Way

607
Artist: WALT SPITZMILLER
Art Director: Walt Spitzmiller
Client: National Kidney Foundation

608
Artist: MARK ENGLISH
Art Director: David G. Foote
Client: United States Postal Service

609
Artist: CONNIE CONNALLY
Art Director: Connie Connally / John Gregory
Agency: Gregory Group
Client: Ralph Lauren / Willow Bend Polo And Hunt Club, Dallas, Texas

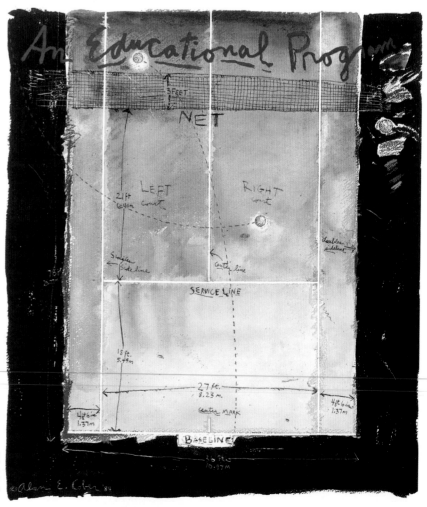

610
Artist: ALAN E. COBER
Art Director: Ellen Wolner
Client: Corchia Wolner

611
Artist: WALT SPITZMILLER   **Art Director:** Walt Spitzmiller   **Client:** Golf / Nuance Graphics

Artist: MARK ENGLISH
Art Director: Shinichiro Tora / Mitsutoshi Hosaka
Client: Hotel Barmen's Association

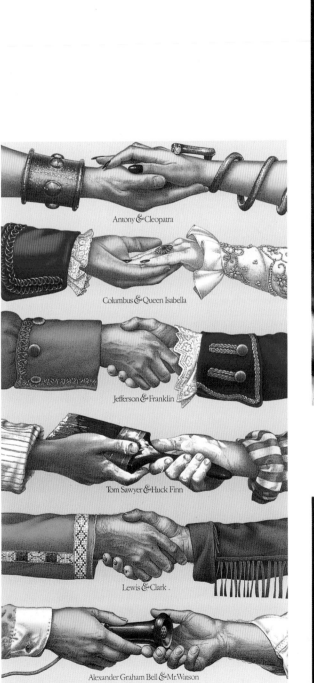

614
Artist: MICK McGINTY
Art Director: Robert M. Fitch
Client: Paper Moon Graphics

613
Artist: MARY LOU WILSON / RICHARD WEHRMAN / VICKI WEHRMAN
Art Director: Mike Fountain
Agency: Hutchins / Y&R
Client: Chase / Lincoln 1st Bank

615
Artist: GEORGE MOATS
Art Director: Steve Carter
Client: Hallmark Cards, Inc.

616
Artist: GARY HEAD
Client: Hallmark Cards, Inc.

617
Artist: MARK ENGLISH
Art Director: Bill Erlacher
Client: Mark English

618
Artist: PETER COX
Art Director: Craig Bernhardt
Client: W.R. Grace

619

Artist: MARGARET CUSACK   Art Director: J. Porter   Client: Yankee Publishing Company

620
Artist: DANIEL SCHWARTZ

621
Artist: NANCY LAWTON
Art Director: Bennett Robinson
Client: H.J. Heinz Company

622

Artist: MELINDA MAY SULLIVAN   Art Director: Melinda May Sullivan   Client: Hotel Meridien, San Francisco

623
Artist: ATTILA HEJJA
Art Director: Alice Price
Client: United States Air Force

626
Artist: REGAN DUNNICK
Art Director: Bruce Blalock
Client: Muse Air Monthly

624
Artist: ATTILA HEJJA
Art Director: Ron Hill
Client: Grumann Aerospace Corporation

625
Artist: ATTILA HEJJA   Art Director: Robert Schulman   Client: National Aeronautics & Space Administration

627
Artist: ROGER HUYSSEN   Art Director: John Berg   Client: Roger Huyssen

628
Artist: BRIAN DAVID MOOSE
Art Director: Dick Oden
Client: FM 88 / KLON

629
Artist: ROBERT HEINDEL
Art Director: Barbara Loveland
Client: Herman Miller Corporation

630
Artist: JUDY PEDERSEN   Art Director: Craig Bernhardt / Janice Fudyma   Client: General Foods Corporation

631
Artist: PAUL MELIA
Art Director: Gene Vauard
Client: General Tire

632
Artist: DOUG JOHNSON   Art Director: Bryan Birch   Agency: Daily & Associates   Client: Armor All Products

633

Artist: SCOTT REYNOLDS   Client: Scott Reynolds

634

Artist: EUGENE MIHAESCO   Art Director: Betsy Halliday   Client: Equitable Group & Health

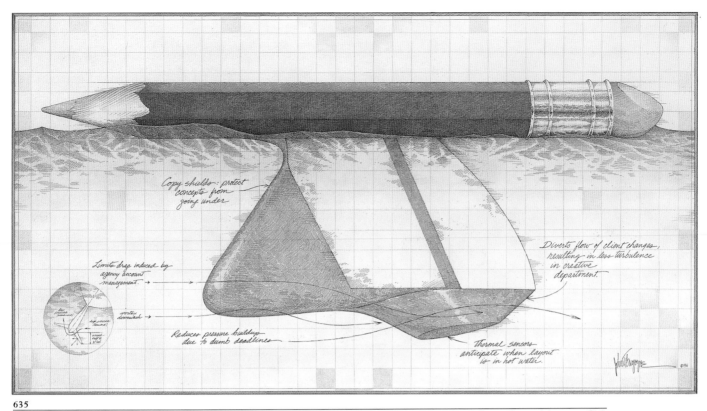

635

Artist: JOHN T. BURGOYNE   Art Director: Bryan McPeak   Agency: Leonard Monahan Saabye   Client: Greater Boston Advertising Club

636

Artist: KAM MAK
Art Director: Bill Kobasz / Richard Wilde
Client: School Of Visual Arts / Master Eagle Family Of Companies

637

Artist: DAVID GROVE
Art Director: Steve Horman
Client: Mercedes-Benz Of North America, Inc.

638
Artist: ROGER T. DeMUTH   Client: Roger T. DeMuth

639
Artist: GREG COUCH
Art Director: Steve Romm
Client: Romm-Lande International Arts, Limited

640
Artist: JOYCE KITCHELL
Art Director: Dennis Gillaspy / Cheryl Woods
Client: Joyce Kitchell / Richard Salzman

641
Artist: BOB BASS

642

Artist: BOB CONGE   Art Director: Bob Conge   Client: Memorial Art Gallery, Rochester, New York

643
Artist: LYNN BYWATERS FERRIS
Art Director: Mary Louise Baker
Client: Sunrise Publications

644
Artist: LAURA CORNELL
Art Director: Don Dame
Client: Image Design / Windemere Press

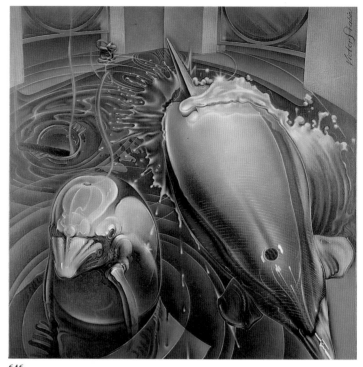

645
Artist: JOHN DYESS
Art Director: Jim Hennessy
Client: Moog Automotive

646
Artist: VICTOR STABIN
Art Director: Victor Stabin
Client: Enterprize Press

647
Artist: JOHN F. WAHL   Art Director: John F. Wahl   Client: Save The Manatee Committee

Artist: KENT WILLIAMS   Client: Kent Williams

Artist: ABE ECHEVARRIA   Client: Abe Echevarria

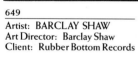

649
Artist: BARCLAY SHAW
Art Director: Barclay Shaw
Client: Rubber Bottom Records

651
Artist: PETER LISIESKI
Client: Peter Lisieski

652
Artist: TIM RAGLIN
Art Director: Tim Raglin
Client: Sunrise Publications

653
Artist: TIM RAGLIN   Art Director: Tim Raglin   Client: Sunrise Publications

654
Artist: JOHN COLLIER
Art Director: Shinichiro Tora
Client: Hotel Barmen's Association

655
Artist: HOWARD POST   Art Director: Howard Post   Client: Kimball Art Center

656
Artist: KIM BEHM
Art Director: Clarence Alling
Client: Waterloo Recreation & Art Center

657
Artist: DAVID TAYLOR
Art Director: Steve Main
Client: Southwest Forest Industries

Artist: JAMES E. TENNISON

Artist: MARY ANN SULLIVAN

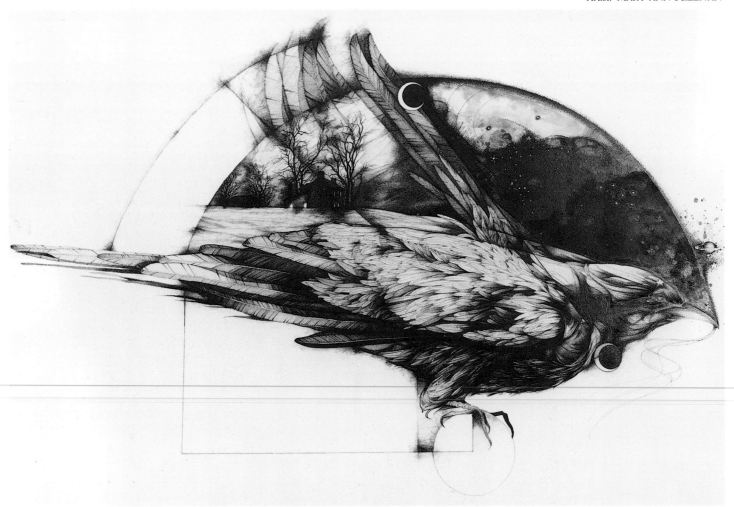

660

Artist: WAYNE TRIMM   Art Director: Robert DeVilleneuve   Client: New York State Return A Gift To Wildlife Contribution /
New York State Department Of Environmental Conservation

661

Artist: SYLVIO REDINGER

662
Artist: JUNE BROCK
Client: Hallmark Cards, Inc.

665
Artist: KEN WALKER
Art Director: Ken Walker
Client: Triad Publications

663
Artist: WENDE L. CAPORALE

664
Artist: MURRAY TINKELMAN   Art Director: Linda Berg   Agency: Rumrill Hoyte   Client: Remington

666
Artist: RICHARD MANTEL
Art Director: Karen Starkey
Client: United States Information Agency

667
Artist: HENRIK DRESCHER
Art Director: Lucille Tenazas
Agency: Harmon Kemp, Inc.
Client: International Paper Company

668
Artist: ROY PENDELTON

INDEX

xvi

INDEX

INDEX

INDEX

INDEX

AGENCIES

SOCIETY OF ILLUSTRATORS MEMBERSHIP

Abbett, Robert
Abel, Raymond
Accornero, Franco
Adams, Jeanette
Adler, Kermit
Adorney, Charles
Albright, Nina
Alexander, James
Alexander, Martha
Alexander, Paul
Allen, Betty H.
Allen, Patricia J.
Allen, Thomas B.
Altekruse, Max
Ambler, Louise
Ameijide, Raymond
Ammirati, Carlo
Andersen, Roy
Anderson, Lyman
Anderson, Richard
Anthony, Al
Anthony, Robert
Arevalo, Walter
Aronson, Alice
Asciutto, Mary Anne
Bacon, Paul
Bald, Ken
Barban, John A.
Barbaresi, Nina A.
Barberis, Juan C.
Barkley, James
Barlowe, Wayne
Barron, Don
Barry, James E.
Bauer, Geraldine
Bender, Gerald D.
Bennett, Brad
Benney, Robert
Benton, Jr., Harrison E.
Berd, Elliot
Berenson, Richard
Berge, James
Berkey, John C.
Berkley, Sy
Bermingham, David
Bernstein, Samuel
Berran, Robert
Berry, Park
Berte, June Allard
Bertolami, Peter
Birmingham, Lloyd P.
Bjorklund, Charles R.
Blair, Bruce
Blattner, Robert H.
Blickenstaff, Wayne K.
Bliok, Leo
Blossom, David
Boddy, Joseph
Bode, Robert
Bogorad, Alan Dale
Bolger, William F.
Bomar, Walter
Bonavita, Donna M.
Bonvino, Michael
Booth, George W.
Bossert, William
Bouffard, John J.
Bowie, Effie
Bowler, Jr., Joseph
Boyd, Douglas
Brackett, Ward
Bralds, Braldt
Bramwell, Randolph
Brandon, Elinore
Brauer, Fred J.
Bridges, Victor
Brindle, Melbourne
Brison, Guy

Brodner, Steve
Brodsky, Ed
Brooks, Andrea
Brooks, Joe
Brooks, Walter
Brown, Daniel J.
Brown, James T.
Brown, Marbury Hill
Brown, Michael David
Brown, Robert
Bugzesten, Ruth
Burgoyne, John
Burns, Charles
Busch, Ronald
Butcher, Lawrence
Cagle, Daryl
Calabrese, Nick
Calaustro, Jr., Braulio
Calle, Paul
Calman, Mel
Campbell, Alice
Campbell, Ronald
Campbell, Stuart
Caniff, Milton
Canniff, Bryan
Capone, Anthony J.
Caram, Raymond
Carr, Barbara
Carr, Charles Noell
Carter, Charles Henry
Cassler, Carl
Castenir, Ralph
Catalano, Al
Cavanagh, Tom
Chaite, Alexander E.
Channell, John W.
Charles, Milton
Charmatz, Bill
Chase, Hermione Palmer
Chaykin, Howard
Chilly, John
Church, Marilyn
Ciardiello, Joseph
Clarke, Grace D.
Clemente, Thomas Frank
Clifford, Judy Dean
Clinton, Brian
Closi, Victor J.
Cober, Alan E.
Cohen, Gil
Combs, Robert Mason
Conge, Bob
Conlon, William J.
Conn, Arthur
Connell, Hugh
Connolly, Howard
Connolly, Joseph
Consor, James Bowman
Content, Dan
Cooper, Cheryl
Cooper, Mario
Copeland, Arnold J.
Cornell, Jeffrey W.
Corvington, Mark
Cosgrove, Jerry L.
Counihan, Gerald T.
Courtland, William
Cox, Peter
Cox, Robert
Craft, Kinuko
Cramer, Ph.D., D.L.
Crawford, Tad
Crockett, Linda
Crofut, Bob
Crouse, Danny
Crowell, James
Crowley, Donald V.
Crozier, Robert

Crump, Frank
Csatari, Joseph
Cuevas, Robert J.
Cumings, Arthur
Cummings, Coco
Cunningham, Robert M.
Dacey, Bob
D'Alelio, Jane
D'Alessio, Gregory
D'Andrea, Bernard
Daily, Don
Dallison, Ken
Daly, Tom
Darling, Lois
Davidian, Anna
Davidson, Everett
Davies, Ken
Davis, Bob A.
Davis, Jack
Davis, Jeff
Davis, Marion
Davis, Marshall
Davis, Paul
Davisson, Zita
De Cesare, John
Declercq, Gilbert
Del Rey, Lester
Della-Piana, Elissa
Demarest, Robert J.
Deschamps, Robert
Descombes, Roland J.
Desmond, Robert F.
Deverin, Daniele
Devino, Frank
Devlin, Harry
Dewey, Ken
Dickerson, James
Di Fate, Vincent
Digianni, John
Dillon, Diane
Dillon, Leo
Dittrich, Dennis
Dobbins, Dwight
Dohanos, Stevan
Dolwick, William A.
Donner, Carol
Doolittle, Melanie
Duffy, William R.
Duillo, Elaine
Dula, William
Dumm, Edwina
Dyekman, James E.
Dystel, Oscar
Dziurlikowski, Thomas
Eagle, Eugene
Eaton, L. Daniel
Effron, Barbara
Ehrhardt, Eleanor
Einsel, Naiad
Einsel, Walter
Eisenberg, Monroe
Eisenstein, Ruth
Eisman, Arthur
Eisner, Norman
Ellis, Dean
Elton, Wallace W.
Emmett, Bruce
Engel, Mort
English, Mark
Ennis, John
Epstein, Lorraine
Erikson, Rolf
Erlacher, Bill
Ermoyan, Arpi
Evans, John Stuart
Falcone, Allen C.
Fass, Harry
Feagans, Thomas I.

Federico, Helen
Feinen, Jeffrey F.
Fennimore, Linda
Ferguson, M. Carr
Ferguson, William Wallace
Ferris, Keith
Fetzer, Craig J.
Fiore, Barbara M.
Fiore, Peter M.
Fisher, Gordon
Fisher, Leonard E.
Fitzgerald, John E.
Flanagan, John
Fletcher, William
Flory, Verdon
Forbes, Bart J.
Forbes, Colin
Foreman, Robert
Fortunato, Al
Forzaglia, John J.
Foster, Robert
Fowler, Eric
Francis, Judy
Frank, Robert
Frankfurt, Stephen O.
Fraser, Betty
Frater, Hal
Frazer, William, L.
Freeman, Fred
Freitag, Samuel
Friedland, Lewis
Frith, Michael K.
Froom, Georgia
Fuchs, Bernard
Fujikawa, Gyo
Fujita, Makoto
Fujita, S. Neil
Gaadt, George S.
Galli, Stanley W.
Gallo, Bill
Galub, Meg
Gamache, John
Garland, Michael
Garn, Dunewald Doris
Gaydos, John
Gayler, Anne
Gehm, Charles C.
George, Robert U.
Gersten, Gerry
Gillot, Carol
Ginsburg, Max
Giordano, Richard
Girard, Samuel
Gittelson, Anders
Glanzman, Louis S.
Glass, Charles
Glattauer, Ned
Gleason, Paul M.
Glick, Judith
Glissmeyer, Garry W.
Gold, Bill
Golden, Allen
Goldstein, Frances
Golton, Glen
Goodman, Adrienne
Gordon, Barbara
Gossett, Milton
Goudeau, Cleven
Graber, Norman
Graham, Mariah
Grant, A. Leigh
Grau, Julie
Gray, George
Green, Anita
Greenblatt, Eunice
Greene, Darrel
Greenhalgh, Robert F.
Greenwald, Herbert

Gregori, Leon
Grider, Dick
Grien, Anita
Grimes, Rick
Grinthal Fuhrmann, Elaine
Gromoll, Kim
Grote, Richard
Groth, John
Grothkopf, Chad M.
Grove, David
Gruppo, Nelson
Guggenheimer, Charles S.
Guzzi, George
Haber, Zelda
Hafner, Marylin
Hainline, Wallace F.
Haley, Richard J.
Hall, Bruce W.
Hall, Deborah Ann
Hall, H. Tom
Hallenbeck, Pomona
Hamilton, Edward
Hamilton, Richard
Hampson, Albert W.
Hampton, Blake
Hamrick, Chuck
Handler, Murray R.
Handville, Robert T.
Hankins, David
Hantman, Carl E.
Hardaway, Ronald H.
Hardy, Neil
Harris, James R.
Harris, Robert G.
Hart, Veronica
Hartman, Bill
Hashimoto, Hirokazu
Hatton, Enid Vaune
Hawes, Charles M.
Hawkins, Jr., Arthur
Healy, Deborah
Hedin, Donald M.
Heindel, Robert
Hejja, Attila
Helck, Peter
Heller, Ruth
Helzer, James A.
Henderson, David F.
Herald, Robert S.
Hermann, Alfred E.
Heron, Joseph E.
Herrick, Ira
Hildebrandt, Gregory J.
Hines, Jack
Hinojosa, Albino R.
Hofmann, Ginnie
Hoie, Claus
Holeywell, Arnold
Hooks, Mitchell
Hortens, Walter
Hosner, William
Hotchkiss, Wesley G.
Huerta, Gerard
Hull, Cathy
Hunt, Peter F.
Huyssen, Roger
Ilsley, Velma
Inouye, Carol
Ishmael, Woodi
Iskowitz, Joel
Jaffee, Allan
James, Bill
Jamison, John
Jankovitz, Frank
Jasper, Jacqueline Ann
Jensen, Enola G.
Johnson, Alfred
Johnson, B.E.

Johnson, Cecile
Johnson, Don
Johnson, Doug
Johnson, Evelyne
Johnson, Gordon A.
Johnson, Lewis P.
Johnson, Max D.
Johnston, Don
Jones, Barry L.
Jones, Casey
Jones, George
Jones, Keith Robert
Jones, Robert
Jones, Taylor
Jonson, Jim
Jossel, Leonard
Jossel, Marguerite
Just, Hal
Kadin, Charles B.
Kaestle, David
Kahn, Harvey
Kalback, Jerry A.
Kamen, Jack
Kamhi, Jack
Kammer, William
Kaloustian, Rosanne
Karl, Gerald T.
Karlin, Bernard
Kastel, Roger
Katinas, Jr., Charles C.
Kaufman, Joe
Kaufman, Max R.
Keefe, Daniel
Kelvin, George V.
Kemble, John S.
Kemper, Bud
Kendrick, Dennis
Kenny, Charlotte
Kent, Albert J.
Kessler, Leonard
Kidd, Steven R.
Kidder, Harvey
Kietz, Alvin
Kimmelman, Phil
King, Jean Callan
King, Gregory N.
King, Stanley
Kinstler, Everett Ray
Kirchoff, Morris A.
Kirk, Charles
Klavins, Uldis
Klein, David
Klein, Donald
Koenigsberg, Marvin
Kohfield, Richard
Kokinos, Tony
Koslow, Howard
Kossin, Sanford
Kowalski, Raymond
Kramer, Dick
Kretschman, Karin
Kristoff, Jeri
Krush, Beth
Krush, Joseph H.
Kubista, John
Kuhlman, William A.
Kunstler, Mort
Kurzweil, Hannah
La Grone, Roy E.
La Pick, John
Lacano, Frank
Lachowicz, Cheryl
Lamacchia, Frank
Lamarque, Abril
Lander, Jane
Landi, Joseph O.
Lane, Leslie
Lapham, Robert

SOCIETY OF ILLUSTRATORS MEMBERSHIP

Lapsley, Robert
Larkin, David
Larson, Esther
Laukhuf, Lawrence A.
Lavin, Robert
Lawrence, Kathy
Lawrence, Lydia
Lazzaro, Victor A.
Lebenson, Richard A.
Lee, Bill
Lee, Nan
Lee, Robert J.
Lee, Tom
Lee, Warren E.
Leggett, Barbara
Leifer, Martin
Leitstein, Harold
Leone, Leonard P.
Lettick, Birney A.
Lewin, Robert L.
Light, Eugene
Lika, Arthur
Linkhorn, Forbes
Lisieski, Peter A.
Liskin, Elliot
Lively, Alton L.
Livingston, Robert Crawford
Llewellyn, William J.
Locke, Nonnie
Long, Charles A.
Longtemps, Kenneth
Loomis, Henry R.
Lorenz, Albert
Lott, George
Lotta, Tom
Lovell, Tom
Lowry, Alfred
Lubey, Richard
Lunde, Thomas R.
Lupo, Dom
Lustig, Loretta E.
Lutz, William J.
Luzak, Dennis
Lyall, Dennis
Lynch, Donald C.
Lyons, Ellen G.
Lyster Armstrong, Susan
Macaulay, Mary
MacDonald, John D.
MacDonald, Robert
MacFadyen, Cornelia
Magagna, Anna Marie
Makris, Nancy L.
Mandel, Bette
Mandel, Saul
Manger, Nina
Mangiat, Jeffrey
Manham, Allan
Maniere, James L.
Marchetti, Louis J.
Marci, Anita
Marcus, Helen
Marinelli, Jack
Marmaras, John S.
Martinez, John R.
Marx, Marcia
Marxer, Donna
Mason, Fred R.
Mattelson, Marvin
Mawicke, Tran
Mayes, Herbert R.
Mayo, Frank
Mays, Maxwell
Mazoujian, Charles J.
McCaffery, Janet
McCall, Robert
McCollum, Rick
McConnell, Gerald

McDaniel, Jerry
McDermott, John R.
McDowell, Lynn Baynon
McEntire, Larry
McGinnis, Robert E.
McIntosh, Jon
McKissick, Randall
McLean, Wilson
McMahon, Eileen
McMullan, James
McNeely, Tom
McPheeters, Neal
McVicker, Charles
Mee, William
Meglin, Nick
Meisel, Ann
Meltzoff, Stanley
Mendelsohn, Michael
Mendez, Toni
Mendola, Joe
Merrill, Abby
Metcalf, Roger K.
Meyer, Gary
Meyer, Susan E.
Meyers, Newton
Milbourn, Pat
Miller, Claudia
Miller, Don
Miller, Phillip
Millington, John
Milne, Jonathan
Minor, Wendell
Miranda, Michael P.
Mistretta, Andrea
Mitchell, Robert L.
Mogel, Leonard
Moodie, John A.
Moreland, Marylee
Morgan, Jacqui
Morrill, Jr., Richard D.
Morrison, William L.
Moscarello, Robert A.
Moschetti, Frank J.
Moshier, Harry
Moss, Donald F.
Moss, Geoffrey
Moss, Tobias
Mott, Herb
Munce, Howard
Munson, Donald
Murley, Malcolm L.
Murphy, John Cullen
Muth, Donald W.
Mutz, Marie
Myers, Lou
Nagoka, Shusei
Najaka, Marlies Merk
Napoli, Augie
Neail, Pamela R.
Neale, Russell
Negron, William
Neher, Fred
Neibart, Wally
Nelson, Carrie Boone
Nessim, Barbara
Netter, M.D., Frank H.
Newborn, Milton
Newman, Frederick R.
Newman, George
Nichol, Richard J.
Noda, Ko
Noonan, Julia
Norem, Earl H.
Noring, Soren
North, Russell C.
Notarile, Chris
Oberheide, Heide
Oh, Jeffrey

Ordan, Jay
Osonitsch, Robert
Osyczka, Bohdan D.
Otnes, Fred
Paces, Zlata
Packer, A. Shore
Paine, Howard
Palmer, Thomas J.
Palulian, Dickran
Parios, Arnold
Park, William B.
Parker, Ed
Parker, Jacques
Parker, Nancy W.
Pasquini, Eric
Paugh, Tom
Payne, George
Peak, Robert
Pearlman, Robert E.
Pecoraro, Charles
Pecoraro, Patricia
Pedersen, B. Martin
Pedersen, Henry M.
Pepper, Brenda
Pepper, Robert
Pereida, Ralph, J.
Perrone, Angelo A.
Pertchik, Harriet
Petro, Joseph V.
Philadelphia College of Art
Phillips, Robert
Pike, Jay Scott
Pimsler, Alvin J.
Pinkney, Jerry
Pisano, Alfred
Plotkin, Barnett
Polenberg, Myron
Popko, Stan
Popp, Walter
Porter, George
Portner, George
Portner, Richard
Portuesi, Louis
Pozefsky, Carol
Prato, Rodica
Pratt Institute
Prentice, John F.
Prestopino, Robert
Price, Alice
Privitello, Michael
Prusmack, Jon
Purdom, William S.
Putt, Glenna
Pyle, Willis A.
Queyroy, Anny
Quon, Mike
Radice, Judith G.
Raglin, Timothy C.
Rainer, Andrea
Ramsay
Ramus, Mike
Rapp, Gerald M.
Raymond, Frank
Redin, Scott Regis
Reed, Robert D.
Reed, Walt
Reininghaus, Ruth
Renfro, Ed
Rey, Marilyn
Reynolds, Keith
Reynolds, Scott
Rhode Island School of Design
Richards, Irene D.
Richards, Linda
Richards, Walter D.
Ritter, Arthur D.
Rixford, Ellen
Robbins, Lisa

Rockmore, Julian A.
Rogers, Howard
Rogers, Warren
Rogoff, Herbert
Roman Helen
Romary, Jr., Alfred J.
Roseman, Mill
Rosenbaum, Harry
Rosenfeld, Mort
Rosier, Lydia
Ross, Alexander
Ross, Barry
Ross, Gordon
Rossi, Joseph O.
Rossin, Lester
Roth, Arnold
Rothovius, Iska
Rowe, Charles
Rudenjak, Phyllis
Rudd, Greg
Sacks, Beverly
Sacks, Cal
Sacks, Julie D.
Sacks, Shelly
Sahni, Tiia Taks
Saks, Robert A.
Sanjulian, Manuel P.
Santore, Charles
Saphore, Athena
Sass, Sidney
Sauber, Rob
Saylor, Steven S.
Schaare, Harry J.
Schallack, Augie
Schelling, George L.
Schleinkofer, David
Schmeck, Heidi L.
Schneider, William
Schoenherr, John C.
School of Visual Arts
Schorr, Kathy S.
Schorr, Todd
Schreck, John
Schulman, Lowell M.
Schultz, Eileen Hedy
Schwartz, Daniel
Schwarz, Jill K.
Scianna, Cosimo
Scott, John W.
Seaver, Jeff
Seiden, Art
Seidler, Ned M.
Selby, Robert
Sharpe, James C.
Shaw, Barclay
Shaw, Wm. Theodore
Shealy, George A.
Shearer, Julie E.
Shilstone, Arthur
Shoemaker, Alan
Shook, Euclid
Shore, Robert
Sidebotham, Jack
Siegel, Leo Dink
Silber, Maurice
Silverman, Robert
Simard, Claude
Simon, A. Christopher
Sinagra, Attilio
Skypeck, George L.
Smith, Douglas B.
Smith, Gail
Smith, Marilyn A.
Smith, Robert S.
Smith, Stanley
Smith, Stephen
Smollin, Michael J.

Sneider, Kenneth P.
Sochis, Reba
Soileau, Hodges
Soldwedel, Kipp
Solie, John Andrew
Solomon, Richard
Sowinski, Walter D.
Spanfeller, James
Spector, Joel
Spiak, Sharon
Spitzmiller, Walter A.
Spohn, Cliff
Spollen, Christopher J.
Stanton, Mindy Phelps
Stasolla, Mario L.
Steadham, Richard
Steadman, Evan T.
Stech, Dave
Stein, Harve
Steinbrenner, Karl H.
Sterrett, Jane
Stevenson, James R.
Stillerman, Roberta
Stirnweis, Shannon
Stone, David K.
Stone, Sylvia
Storch, Otto
Stretton, Gertrude
Stromberg, Mike
Suh, Jeongin
Sumichrast, Jozef
Swanson, Robert
Sweeney, Brian M.
Taback, Simms
Takahashi, Kyo
Tanabe, Masakazu
Tanen, Norman
Tanenbaum, Robert
Tankersley, Paul Clark
Tanner, Bert
Tardiff, Melissa
Tauss, Herbert
Tauss, Jack
Taylor, Dahl
Teaford, Lee
Teason, William I.
Tennant, Craig
Tennison, John
Tepper, Matthew
Tepper, Saul
Terreson, Jeffrey
Teringo, J. Robert
Theryoung, Richard
Thomas, Maurice
Thompson, Eugene
Thompson, J. Bradbury
Thompson, John
Thompson, Kenneth W.
Thurston, Jack
Tinkelman, Murray
Tommasino, David
Tora, Shinichiro
Townsend, Jr., Lloyd
Troop, Miriam
Trooper, David
Trowbridge, Susan B.
Tsugami, Kyuzo
Unruh, Jack
Usher, David P.
Valla, Victor
Van Buren, Raeburn
Van Rynbach, Iris
Vebell, Edward
Vernaglia, Michael
Vero, Radu
Vetromile, Alfred G.
Vidal, Hahn
Vizbar, Milda

Von Der Linn, Thomas W.
Wald, Carol
Walker, Mort
Walker, Norman
Wallberg, Susan M.
Walling, Dow
Wapner, Raymond
Watts, Mark
Weber, Jessica M.
Weekly, Helen
Weinberg, Harvey L.
Weisman, Jerome
Weiss, Morris S.
Weithas, Arthur
Wende, Phillip
Wenzel, David T.
Wergeles, Ed
Whelan, Michael R.
Whitcomb, Jon
White, Bernard J.
White, James D.
Whitmore, Coburn
Whyte, Andrew C.
Willbright, Frank
Williams, Paul
Williamson, Mel
Willinger, Kurt
Wilson, George D.
Winkler, Roy
Winter, Donald M.
Witalis, Rupert
Witt, John
Wohlberg, Helen
Wohlberg, Meg
Wohlsen, Sr., Robert S.
Wolf, Ann
Wolfe, Jean E.
Wooten, Vernon E.
Yohe, Tom G.
Young, Cliff
Zaino, Carmile S.
Zander, Jack
Ziemienski, Dennis
Ziering, Bob
Zimmerman, Marie
Zinggeler, Jeff
Zuckerman, Paul

JOEL SPECTOR

PETER FIORE

MENDOLA LTD. · 420 LEXINGTON AVENUE, NEW YORK, N.Y. 10170 · (212) 986-5680

JOHN SOLIE

MENDOLA LTD. · 420 LEXINGTON AVENUE, NEW YORK, N.Y. 10170 · (212) 986-5680

DAVID SCHLEINKOFER

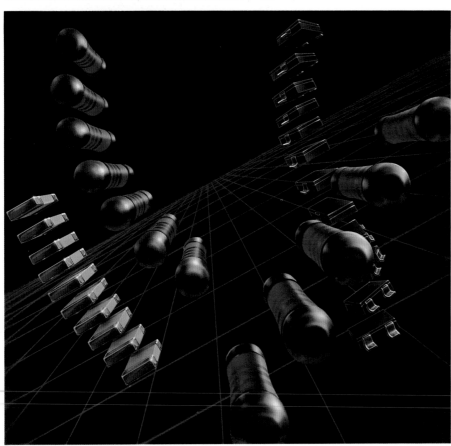

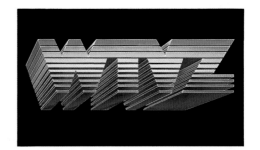

JEFFREY LYNCH

MENDOLA LTD. · 420 LEXINGTON AVENUE, NEW YORK, N.Y. 10170 · (212) 986-5680

JEFFREY TERRESON

MITCHELL HOOKS

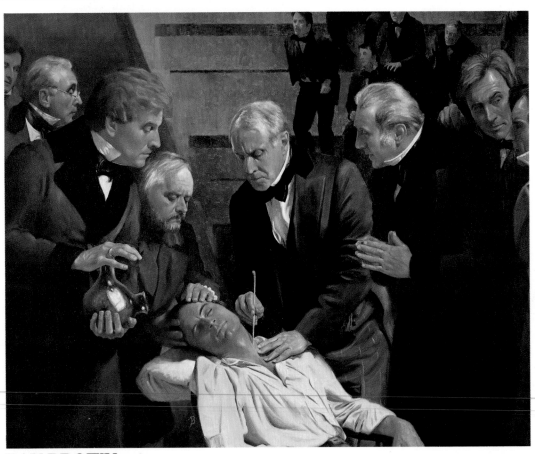

DAN BROWN

MENDOLA LTD. · 420 LEXINGTON AVENUE, NEW YORK, N.Y. 10170 · (212) 986-5680

ATTILA HEJJA

MENDOLA LTD. · 420 LEXINGTON AVENUE, NEW YORK, N.Y. 10170 · (212) 986-5680

PAUL ALEXANDER

PAUL TANKERSLEY

MENDOLA LTD. · 420 LEXINGTON AVENUE, NEW YORK, N.Y. 10170 · (212) 986-5680

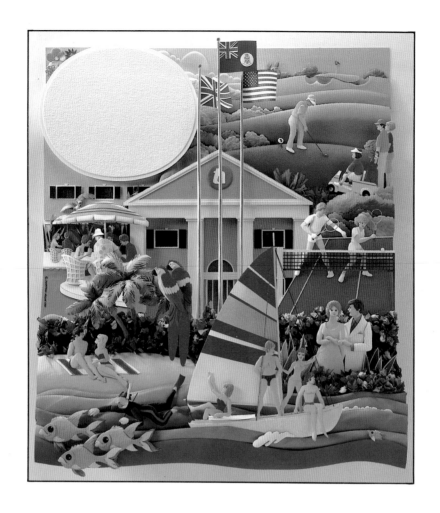

JONATHAN MILNE

MENDOLA LTD. · 420 LEXINGTON AVENUE, NEW YORK, N.Y. 10170 · (212) 986-5680

DAVID BLOSSOM

DONNA DIAMOND

GREG RUDD

KEN DEWEY

MENDOLA LTD. · 420 LEXINGTON AVENUE, NEW YORK, N.Y. 10170 · (212) 986-5680

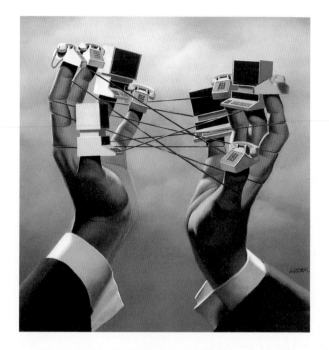

DENNIS LUZAK

MENDOLA LTD. · 420 LEXINGTON AVENUE, NEW YORK, N.Y. 10170 · (212) 986-5680

JEFFREY MANGIAT

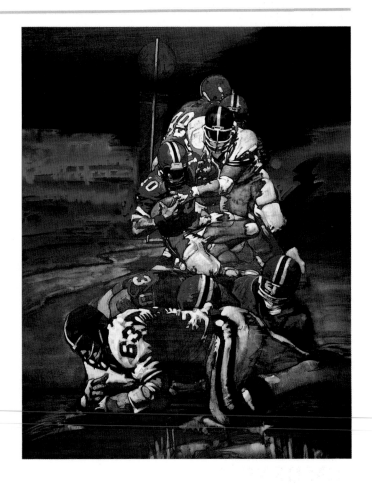

JIM CAMPBELL

MENDOLA LTD. · 420 LEXINGTON AVENUE, NEW YORK, N.Y. 10170 · (212) 986-5680

JIM DENEEN

MENDOLA LTD. · 420 LEXINGTON AVENUE, NEW YORK, N.Y. 10170 · (212) 986-5680

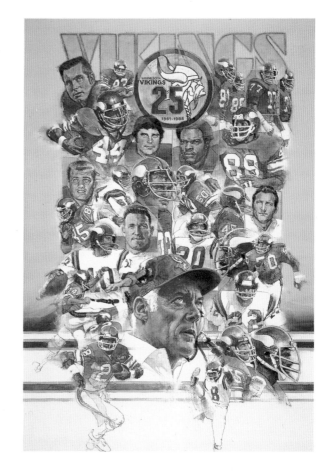

CLIFF SPOHN

DAVID HENDERSON

MENDOLA LTD. · 420 LEXINGTON AVENUE, NEW YORK, N.Y. 10170 · (212) 986-5680

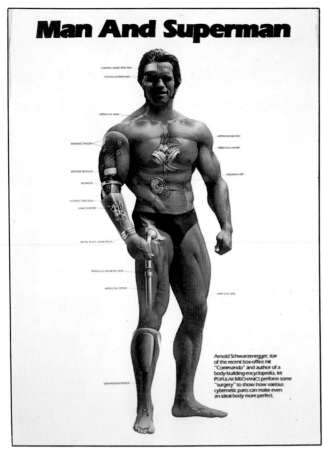

Man And Superman

MICHAEL KOESTER

CHRISTINE FROMENTIN

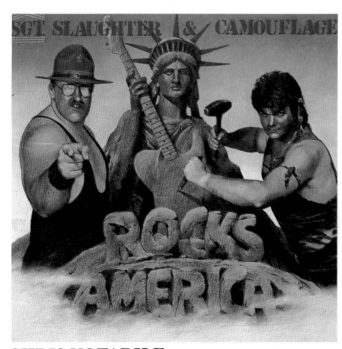

CHRIS NOTARILE

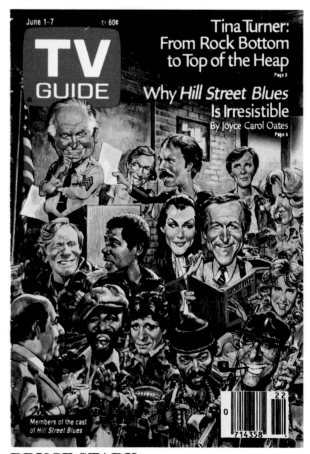

BRUCE STARK

MENDOLA LTD. · 420 LEXINGTON AVENUE, NEW YORK, N.Y. 10170 · (212) 986-5680

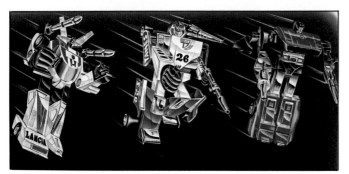

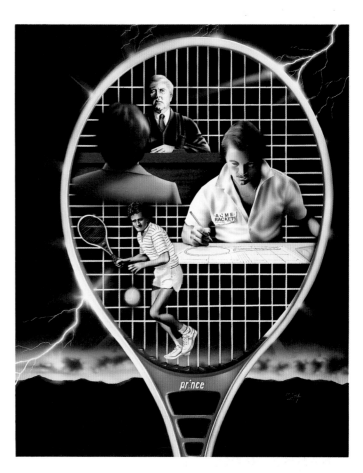

MARK WATTS

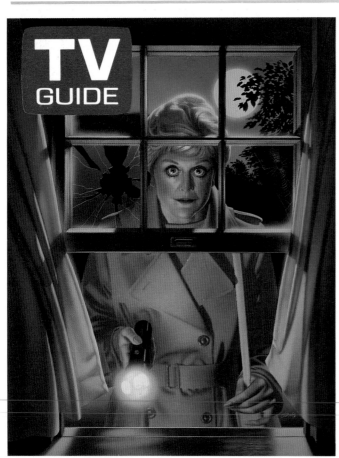

DAVID JARVIS

MENDOLA LTD. · 420 LEXINGTON AVENUE, NEW YORK, N.Y. 10170 · (212) 986-5680

BARRY MORGEN

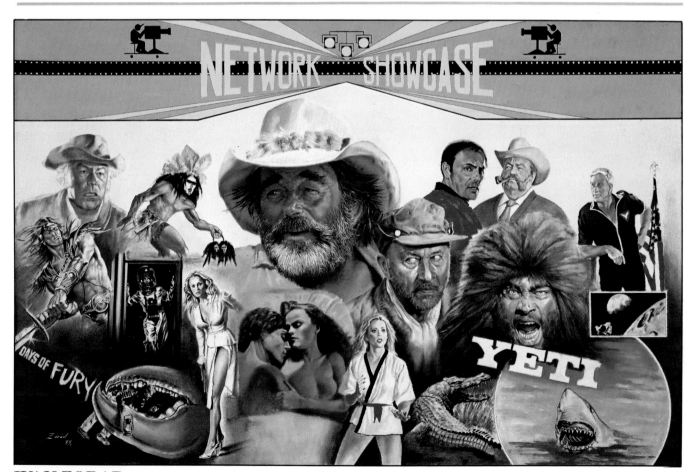

IVAN ZORAD

MENDOLA LTD. · 420 LEXINGTON AVENUE, NEW YORK, N.Y. 10170 · (212) 986-5680

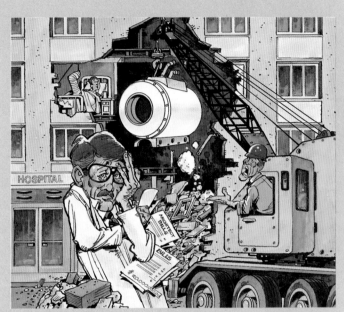

BOB JONES

KIPP SOLDWEDEL

PAUL JENNIS

ROBERT BERRAN

MENDOLA LTD. · 420 LEXINGTON AVENUE, NEW YORK, N.Y. 10170 · (212) 986-5680

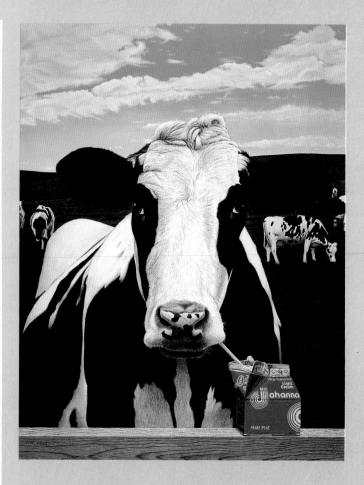

JON ELLIS

TED MICHENER

MENDOLA LTD. · 420 LEXINGTON AVENUE, NEW YORK, N.Y. 10170 · (212) 986-5680

RAPIDOGRAPH®
. . .pen-and-ink textures by Dan Puffer

It is obvious that Dan Puffer, a metallurgical engineer by profession, has mastered the challenge of his avocation—Rapidograph pen-and-ink drawing. He interprets dramatically the textures of objects in his environment, such as the pitted coral blocks of an unfinished, long-abandoned cathedral on Bermuda, of weathered and saw-marked shingles, of tree bark and grassy fields, of a butterfly and peeling paint.

While the artist's skills are the essential ingredient for this demanding task, the hours of dependable output provided by his Rapidograph pens are equally impressive. Tubular nib (available in 13 line widths) allows the Rapidograph pen to move in any direction on virtually any drawing surface (including acetate and glass) with the ease of, and with even less pressure than pencil, making it far more versatile and less fatiguing to use than crow quill or wing-nib pens. Refillable ink cartridge is another artist-pleasing feature, permitting long, uninterrupted drawing sessions at home or in the field or studio.

The patented DRY DOUBLE-SEAL™ cap keeps ink throughout the

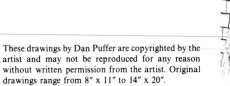

ART

balanced ink-flow system fluid, ready for instant startup and optimum drawing time. No maintenance-plagued gimmicks for sealing or humidifying. Accept no substitutes. Look for the *Koh-I-Noor Rapidograph* on the pen holder to be sure you have the most widely accepted and proven technical pen in the United States and Canada.

"Get-acquainted" packaging (Product No. 3165-BX) offers a special saving with pen/ink combination and your choice of the five most popular Rapidograph line widths. Single pens and pen sets in a number of configurations are also available. Ask your dealer or send the coupon for details: Koh-I-Noor Rapidograph, Inc., Bloomsbury, NJ 08804 (201) 479-4124. In Canada: 1815 Meyerside Dr., Mississauga, Ont. L5T 1B4 (416) 671-0696.

KOH·I·NOOR
RAPIDOGRAPH®

HARVEY KAHN ASSOCIATES, INC.

50 East 50 Street New York, NY 10022   (212) 752-8490
Doug Kahn, Associate

ALAN E. COBER

BOB PEAK

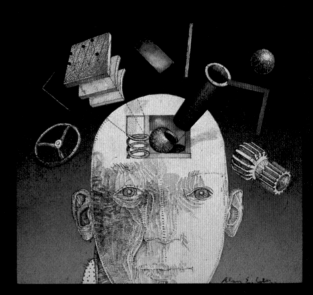

WILSON McLEAN

American Broadcasting Co.
American Express
AT&T
Avis
Bank of America
Borden Inc.
CBS
Celanese
Champion International
Chemical Bank
Citibank
Citicorp
Cullinet
Curtiss-Wright
Datamation Systems Inc.
Digital Equipment
Walt Disney Productions
Dr. Pepper
Eli Lilly
Exxon
Fortune
General Foods
Grumman
Herman Miller, Inc.
Hiram Walker
Hoechst Fibers

Holland American Lines
IBM
Johnson & Johnson
Kinney Corp.
Merrill Lynch
Mobil
Mohawk Paper
Newsweek
New York Telephone
Nikon
Novacor
Oppenheimer
Perdue Inc.
Pioneer Electronics
Radio Corporation of America
Revlon
Scott Paper Co.
Southland Corp.
Southwestern Bell
Time
United Telecom
Universal Pictures
U.S. Postal Service
S. D. Warren
Western Union
Ziff-Davis Publishing Co.

GERRY GERSTEN

NICHOLAS GAETANO

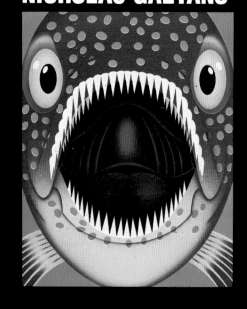

ISADORE SELTZER

BERNIE FUCHS

HARVEY KAHN ASSOCIATES, INC.

50 East 50 Street New York, NY 10022   (212) 752-8490
Doug Kahn, Associate

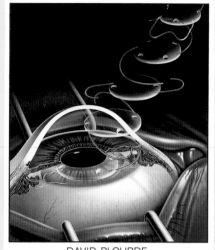

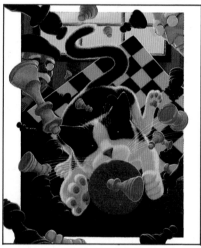

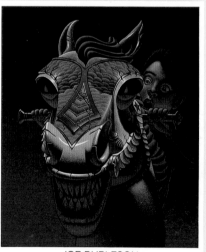

William Hosner
Illustrations

450 West Fort Street
Detroit, Michigan 48226
313•962•0405

Linda Crockett

Illustrations

796 East 222 Street
Euclid, Ohio 44123
216•261•7031

- Competitive cost
  - Flexibility in production time
    - Knowledge of sales reps
      - Service and fine quality
        - Financial stability

Can you expect all of these from your printer ?

The Society of Illustrators has come to us since its annual book, "Illustrators 23."

 DAI NIPPON is ready to serve you. You can get on the spot consultation from professional salesman.

Duane Michals photographing the faculty of The Illustrators Workshop, Paris

Photo sequence by Duane Michals

Robert Heindel, Fred Otnes, Robert Peak, Alan E. Cober, Bernie Fuchs, Mark English

SIX
OF
AMERICA'S
GREATEST
ILLUSTRATORS
INVITE
YOU
TO
JOIN
THEM
EVERY
YEAR
SOMEWHERE

The
Illustrators
Workshop

The programs feature in-depth slide presentations by the faculty and guests, one-on-one portfolio reviews, workshops by the faculty, open discussion groups, a live assignment for a major paper company, and perhaps best of all, plenty of free time to get to know the faculty and guests on a personal basis.

Write for more information.

The Illustrators Workshop
P.O. Box 3447
Noroton, CT 06820 USA
203-655-8394

BILL ERLACHER ARTISTS ASSOCIATES

ARTISTS REPRESENTED

NORMAN ADAMS

DON BRAUTIGAM

MICHAEL DEAS

MARK ENGLISH

ROBERT HEINDEL

STEVE KARCHIN

DICK KREPEL

SKIP LIEPKE

FRED OTNES

DANIEL SCHWARTZ

NORMAN WALKER

211 EAST 51 STREET, NEW YORK, NEW YORK 10022 (212) 755-1365/6 ASSOCIATE: NICOLE EDELL

Artists Representative
KIRCHOFF/WOHLBERG, INC.

866 UNITED NATIONS PLAZA, NEW YORK, NY 10017   212-644-2020
897 BOSTON POST ROAD, MADISON, CT 06443   203-245-7308

JOHN GANNAM, A.N.A. (1907-1965)

OUR TEN COMMANDMENTS of ARTIST REPRESENTATION

1. We represent only artists we believe in and are totally committed to them.

2. We believe in being more than agents and become involved in the *total career* of the artists we represent.

3. We appreciate the problems of the artist and try, whenever possible, to alleviate these problems.

4. We also appreciate the problems of the art director: his client-agency relationship, tight deadlines and budget limitations and try to help him solve these problems whenever we can.

5. We believe in *full representation.* That means taking on only that number of artists that we can fully represent as well as insuring that each artist is non-competitive in style with other artists we represent.

6. We believe in giving *full service* to our artists and to the art director, promptly and professionally. Every client, no matter what the job price, deserves the very best we can offer.

7. We believe in being *flexible.* Business conditions change. The economy rises and falls. Accounts switch. We and our artists must adjust to all changes in order to successfully survive.

8. We believe in always meeting deadlines and always keeping a bargain. We and our artists are only as good as our word and our last job.

9. We believe in *BEING HONEST* at all times. With our artists. With the art director. With ourselves.

10. And finally, we believe in our *profession...* the profession of representing artists. We firmly believe that it is the most exciting and challenging profession anywhere and we are proud to be a part of it.

Barbara Gordon
Associates Ltd.
165 East 32 Street
New York, N.Y. 10016
212-686-3514

Barbara and Elliott Gordon are also co-authors of the book,
"HOW TO SURVIVE IN THE FREE LANCE JUNGLE—A Realistic Plan for Success in Commercial Art". To order, send $9.95, check or money order,
to *EXECUTIVE COMMUNICATIONS INC.* 919 Third Avenue. New York NY 10022

Dramatic savings on Society of Illustrators Annuals

Foremost in the field, the classic Annuals are important additions to any art library—some at half price! Soon to become collectors' items, these award-winning volumes are excellent reference for art directors, educators, students and all artists.

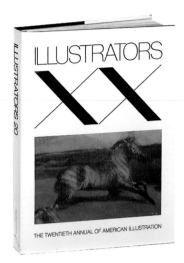

ILLUSTRATORS 20
THE 20th ANNUAL OF AMERICAN ILLUSTRATION
PUBLISHED FOR THE SOCIETY OF ILLUSTRATORS
Edited by Gerald McConnell/Designed by Robert Hallock

Since 1959 the Society of Illustrators has held an Annual National Exhibition of the most outstanding work done each year in the major areas of illustration. Out of thousands of entries submitted, about 500 are selected for exhibition, then compiled into a handsome volume.

This Illustrators 20 edition contains the juried selections and award winners in the Advertising, Editorial, Book, Institutional, Film and Television categories.

A unique record of the social mores and attitudes of the times, this is history seen through the eyes of artists, the most acute observers of all.
ISBN 8038-3420-9
List $29.50   **MSP price $17.95**

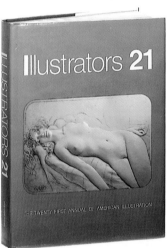

ILLUSTRATORS 21
THE 21st ANNUAL OF AMERICAN ILLUSTRATION
PUBLISHED FOR THE SOCIETY OF ILLUSTRATORS
Edited by Gerald McConnell/Designed by Robert Hallock

Thirty-eight eminent professionals in the graphics industry distilled more than 5,000 entries submitted to the Society of Illustrators Annual Exhibition down to the 586 examples shown in this volume. Covering a wide range of techniques and styles, this book offers a multitude of inspirational ideas for students and educators as well as established professionals.

Included are the illustrations selected as the best in Advertising, Editorial, Book, Institutional and TV/Film categories. ISBN 8038-3427-6
List $35.00   **MSP price $17.95**

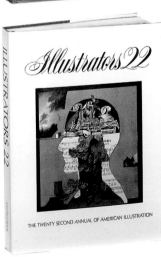

ILLUSTRATORS 22
THE 22nd ANNUAL OF AMERICAN ILLUSTRATION
PUBLISHED FOR THE SOCIETY OF ILLUSTRATORS
Edited by Forbes Linkhorn/Designed by Robert Hallock

Within the pages of this 22nd Annual is a comprehensive collection of exciting talent. These volumes have become standard reference sources for art directors, creative directors and all buyers of illustration.

Included are all the juried selections and award winners from the Society of Illustrators 22nd Annual National Exhibition. Of added interest are capsule biographies and examples of the work of Hall of Fame award winners Howard Chandler Christy, James Montgomery Flagg and Saul Tepper.
ISBN 8038-3433-0
List $37.50   **MSP price $17.95**

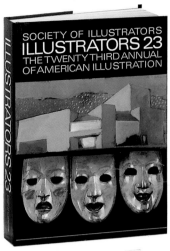

ILLUSTRATORS 23
THE 23rd ANNUAL OF AMERICAN ILLUSTRATION
PUBLISHED FOR THE SOCIETY OF ILLUSTRATORS
Edited by Howard Munce/Designed by Robert Hallock

The skilled and imaginative work of the 337 diverse individuals reproduced in this volume is a silent compliment to the countless talented people—art directors, editors and writers—who worked with them in the commercial chain of command. Included are 591 superb examples of paintings, drawings and dimensional art that appeared in the Society of Illustrators 23rd Annual Exhibition.

In addition to the Advertising, Editorial, Book, Institutional and TV categories is a bonus supplement of 48 illustrations in the Foreign category.
ISBN 8038-3433-0
List $39.95   **MSP price $21.95**

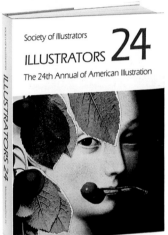

ILLUSTRATORS 24
THE 24th ANNUAL OF AMERICAN ILLUSTRATION
PUBLISHED FOR THE SOCIETY OF ILLUSTRATORS
Edited by Art Weithas/Designed by Robert Hallock

Four distinguished panels of jurors selected these 501 examples of American illustration from thousands of entries of both published and unpublished work: 113 in the Editorial category, 138 in Book, 149 in Advertising and 101 in the Institutional category. Over 160 illustrations are reproduced in full color.

An interesting supplement of the Society of Illustrators' activities, including its Museum of American Illustration, Permanent Collection, Hall of Fame, Annual Scholarship Competition, Exhibitions, Art Auction, and Evening Workshops, appears in this volume. ISBN 0-942604-00-8
List $39.95   **MSP price $21.95**

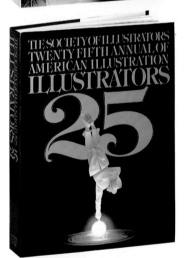

ILLUSTRATORS 25
THE 25th ANNUAL OF AMERICAN ILLUSTRATION
PUBLISHED FOR THE SOCIETY OF ILLUSTRATORS
Edited by Art Weithas/Designed by Robert Anthony

Illustrators 25 is the first issue to be printed entirely in full color!

This magnificent book marks the Silver Anniversary of the Society of Illustrators Annuals. Considered the most outstanding publication of its kind, this series has shown the finest contemporary illustration for the past quarter of a century.

Within the pages of this 440 page volume are over 500 illustrations in the Editorial, Advertising, Book and Institutional categories. ISBN 0-942604-02-4
List $49.95   **MSP price $41.95**

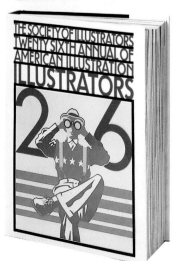

ILLUSTRATORS 26
THE 26th ANNUAL OF AMERICAN ILLUSTRATION
PUBLISHED FOR THE SOCIETY OF ILLUSTRATORS
Edited by Art Weithas/Designed by Robert Anthony

This lavish, full-color volume is the oldest and most prestigious illustration annual on the market. It is an exceptional source of creative ideas and an excellent reference for all who need to see the work of new talents and the new work of old talents. Four panels of notable jurors selected the 551 illustrations in the four categories—Advertising, Editorial, Book and Institutional—from more than 7,500 entries submitted.

A section in front of the book is devoted to the Society of Illustrators Hall of Fame, Hamilton King Award and New Acquisitions of the Society's Permanent Collection. The back section contains information and pictures of the Society's many activities and exhibitions. ISBN 0-942604-05-9   **$49.95**

List title(s) and send check or money order to:
MADISON SQUARE PRESS, INC.
10 East 23rd Street, New York, NY 10010

U.S. sales only: Please add $2.50 handling and postage charge for first book and $1.00 for each book thereafter. New York State residents add 8.25% sales tax.

THE ILLUSTRATOR IN AMERICA 1880·1980

Walt and Roger Reed

SPECIAL LIMITED EDITIONS

**The Society of Illustrators is proud to offer
a limited edition of signed and numbered volumes of
The Illustrator in America 1880-1980 by Walt and Roger Reed.**

Each contains an original work by one of three famous illustrators:
F.R. Gruger   John Held, Jr.   Harry Beckhoff

This special limited edition gives you an original work of art for your collection plus an exquisite volume for your library. Each Gruger, Held and Beckhoff is hand-tipped in on special stock in gilt-edged, handsomely boxed editions of *The Illustrator in America 1880-1980*. All are signed and numbered. Autographed by the authors, every volume also has the purchaser's name embossed in gold on the cover.

The author, Walt Reed, is the preeminent illustration historian who has written volumes on such notables as Harold Von Schmidt, John Clymer and Joseph Clement Coll. With his son Roger, he owns Illustration House, Inc., a gallery devoted entirely to the work of illustrators. Together the Reeds have recorded the lives and

exhibited the works of every important artist from 1880-1980. From early masters like Howard Pyle, Charles Dana Gibson and N.C. Wyeth, to the Golden Days of Frederic Remington, Maxfield Parrish, Norman Rockwell, Stevan Dohanos and, more contemporarily, Bernard Fuchs, Milton Glaser and Brad Holland.

Each decade in the book is introduced by a famous illustrator with comprehensive knowledge of the period. This exciting volume provides historical facts, personality insights and examples by the great illustrators. Our special limited edition provides an opportunity to possess an original illustration by three of the most important artists of the last century.

The deluxe, 9 x 12 editions, containing over 700 illustrations on 352 pages, half in full color, are a complete pictorial and biographical record of the greatest illustrators in America from 1880 to 1980.

F.R. Gruger: approximately 4" x 7"

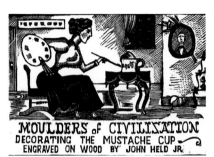

John Held Jr.: actual size 4¾" x 3¼"

Harry Beckhoff: approximately 3" x 2"

250 ORIGINAL F.R. GRUGER DRAW-INGS, estate-signed and numbered, tipped into special, limited editions of THE ILLUSTRATOR IN AMERICA 1880-1980, autographed by Walt and Roger Reed. An illustrator's illustrator, Gruger is on a par with Pyle, Wyeth and Gibson. In the Society of Illustrators Hall of Fame, he is a recognized master.

50 JOHN HELD, JR. WOODBLOCK PRINTS. From a one-of-a-kind edition of 100, these prints are signed by Mrs. John Held, Jr. and tipped into auto-graphed copies of THE ILLUSTRA-TOR IN AMERICA 1880-1980. Harold Ross, famed *New Yorker* editor, commissioned Held to do satirical studies of the Victorian era. This is one of the finest examples.

200 ORIGINAL HARRY BECKHOFF DRAWINGS, signed by the artist and numbered, tipped into special, limited editions of THE ILLUSTRATOR IN AMERICA 1880-1980 and auto-graphed by Walt and Roger Reed. These jewel-like thumbnail sketches contain all the necessary information for the final artwork. Beckhoff is best known for his Damon Runyan characters for *Collier's.*

ALL SPECIAL VOLUMES ARE ELEGANTLY BOXED, AUTOGRAPHED BY THE AUTHORS AND EMBOSSED WITH THE NAME OF THE PURCHASER.

- -

Order Your Copy of THE ILLUSTRATOR IN AMERICA 1880-1980...Today

___*volume(s) of THE ILLUSTRATOR IN AMERICA 1880-1980 by Walt and Roger Reed containing one of 250 original drawings by F.R. GRUGER, hand-tipped on special stock, estate-signed, autographed by the authors, with purchaser's name embossed in gold and handsomely boxed.*

$150.00

___*volume(s) of THE ILLUSTRATOR IN AMERICA 1880-1980 by Walt and Roger Reed containing one of 200 original drawings by HARRY BECKHOFF, hand-tipped on special stock, signed by the artist, autographed by the authors, with purchaser's name embossed in gold and handsomely boxed.*

$75.00

___*volume(s) of THE ILLUSTRATOR IN AMERICA 1880-1980 by Walt and Roger Reed containing one of 100 original woodcuts by JOHN HELD, JR., hand-tipped on special stock, signed by Mrs. John Held, Jr., auto-graphed by the authors, with purchaser's name embossed in gold and handsomely boxed.*

$50.00

___**Plus $2.50 per copy for postage and handling. Please make checks payable to:**

Madison Square Press, Inc.
10 East 23rd Street
New York City, NY 10010

Charge my credit card plus $2.50 per copy for postage and handling.

Check one:

☐ **American Express**

☐ **Visa**

☐ **Master Charge**

Number_____

_____

Exp. date_____

Name _____

Address _____

City _____

State _____ **Zip** _____

Signature _____

New York State residents add 8.25% sales tax.